## About the author

Yvonne Allen, founder and managing director of Yvonne Allen & Associates, Human Relations Consultants (Sydney), has since 1976 provided a unique service for people without partners who want to develop relationships.

Her academic background (BA Psych UNSW) has focused on psychology, communication skills and group processes. Her submission to the Royal Commission on Human Relationships regarding loneliness and alienation in Australian society launched her current career. In 1983 Ms Allen addressed the first annual conference of Marriage & Family Counsellors on 'The Preventive and Therapeutic Implications of an Introduction Service'.

In the course of her work and highly successful seminars, she has not only helped many single people of all ages to understand their needs, but has also built up an immense fund of experience on living without a partner. Her experience, case studies and seminar handbooks provide the basis of this book; her sensitivity, ease of communication and empathy set in apart.

Ms Allen appears regularly on television, radio and in the press, advising single people on ways in which to improve their lives – and seek rewarding partnerships. Ms Allen is 37, and a successful single.

# SUCCESSFULLY
# Single
# SUCCESSFULLY
# YOURSELF

## Yvonne Allen

CEDAR

An imprint of William Heinemann Ltd

Published by Cedar Books
an imprint of
William Heinemann Limited
Michelin House, 81 Fulham Road, London SW3 6RB

LONDON   MELBOURNE   AUCKLAND

Copyright © Yvonne Allen 1987

First published 1987 by
William Heinemann Australia
in association with
René Gordon Pty Ltd
29 Ferdinand Avenue
North Balwyn Vic 3104
Australia

First published in Great Britain 1988

Commissioned and produced by René Gordon Pty Ltd
Designed by Lynda Patullo, Melbourne
Typeset by Savage Type Pty Ltd, Brisbane
Printed and bound in Great Britain by
Richard Clay Ltd, Bungay, Suffolk

ISBN  0  434  11155  4

# CONTENTS

**Some opening words**  1
**Some words of thanks**  5

## PART I FIRST PERSON SINGULAR  7

**Let's get our bearings**  9
Some singular stereotypes  12
Singularly odd?  13
**Why sail life solo?**  15
Single by choice  16
Single because I'm scared  17
The gay option  18
Single through circumstance  18
On the lookout but not looked for  18
Are the odds in your favour?  19
A male shortage  20
The marriage squeeze  20
No one in sight for the fair and bright  21
Some men are also disadvantaged  21
Single but a package  21
Judging a book by its cover  22
**Marriage ... an insecure mooring?**  24
What's gone wrong with marriage?  25
The baby boom generation  26
Who am I without a partner?  26
A different agenda  27
Economic independence  28
Sexual freedom  28
You and me against the world  28
**Sights set on coupledom ... different sex,
different issues**  31
What should little boys be made of and become?  31
... and what about little girls?  32
Man, singular  33
In quest of a breast  34
The recycled male  36
Look to the woman within  37
Learn from living singly  37
**Woman, singular**  38
How can a woman become herself?  39
A good man can be hard to find  40

Superwoman? 41
Can a woman be happy without a mate? 41
Supermum 42
The older woman 43
Some singular lessons 43
**Co-captains ... a new breed of relationship** 45
A new breed of man 47
**The new mythmakers ... a warning** 48
Let's question assumptions 49

# PART II A SINGULAR WORKBOOK 51
**Your expectations** 53
Are you single again? 60
Have you been widowed? 60
Are you separated? 60
Are you single and a parent? 61
Have you always been single? 61
Are you partnered? 63
**Your lifeline** 72
**Where are you now?** 80
How satisfied are you with your life now? 86
What values are important to you? 90
Influences on your life so far 92
Learning from your past relationships 93
**Your epitaph** 97
A review 98

# PART III SOME SINGULAR ISSUES 101
**Responsibility for self** 103
Finding inner security 104
Growth to the end 104
Loneliness 104
Shyness 107
Living singly together 108
**Single and sexual** 110
Some practicalities 111
A sexual scale 113
Sex with strangers 115
Finding satisfaction 116
Single and gay 117

Male and gay 117
… and what about women who are gay? 119
**The issue of issue** 121
Single and a parent 122
Overcoming isolation 123
What about sex? 125
A mother/father figure for my kids 127
**Single again** 128
Widowed 132
Look before you leap again 133
Standing on your own two feet 136
Challenge of the unknown 137
**Single and aged** 140

# PART IV SOME SINGULAR LIVES 143
**Singular examples** 145
**Margo** 146
**Brenda** 157
**Peter** 165
**Diane** 174
**Steve** 179
**A closing thought** 187
Source list 188
Index 189

# SOME OPENING WORDS

When it was first suggested that I write a book on being single I was somewhat taken aback. Although I was single and had lived most of my life without a particular partner, I had doubts about my being the appropriate person. My occupation seemed to contradict the purpose of the project; for many years I have specialised in counselling men and women who would prefer not to be single and I had made it my business to assist them meet a potential mate.

There was a need for a book which addressed the issues of living effectively without a partner, but how could I attempt such a mammoth task? I was continually struggling with the dilemmas of my own life, so what did I have to say?

Yet through my work I have been in a privileged position to gain insights into many of the challenges that confront those who live singly. The men and women who have attended my seminars on making more of a single lifestyle, and my single friends and acquaintances with whom I have debated the issues, were all a rich resource

I could call upon to help me explore some of the issues of being single in the 1980s. So, just as I've always encouraged my clients to stretch themselves, to believe that they can do anything if they really want to, I accepted the challenge and *Successfully Single* was born.

There is a real temptation for people in the field of human relations to tell others what to do and how to live their lives. While their training and experience does give them valuable insights to share, perhaps more importantly they are in a good position to suggest options. In writing this book I see my role more as a source of alternatives and a challenger of accepted ideas than as a supplier of answers. I see your role, as a reader, as equally vital in determining what it is to be successfully yourself and successfully single.

Throughout this book you will be asked to consider questions to which there are no right or wrong answers. By contributing your own thoughts regarding the issues raised, this exploration of what it is to be single will be of your own making, as well as an expression of some of my ideas, insights and experiences.

Through the questions I raise, the suggestions I make, and the options I consider, and from your answers to the exercises I present, you can explore the ways by which you can express your unique potential and create a rich and rewarding life for yourself — be this with or without a partner. I see myself as a catalyst challenging you to make more of your life by inviting you to be, in a very real sense, a co-author of *Successfully Single*.

In Part I, 'First person singular', I ask you to explore with me what it is to be single today. We will consider some of the changes in society over the past decades that have resulted in more people living singly, be this through choice or circumstance. We will look at various stereotypes and consider some of the pressures placed upon the person without a partner to conform to misleading images. We will see that there are very few guidelines to living effectively as a single person and that this in fact makes it easier for us to be ourselves and to determine our own lifepath, if we dare take up the challenge.

In Part II, 'A singular workbook', I take you into a workshop in which several men and women explore what being single means to them in the context of their life experience and the desires they have for the future. Not only are you invited to join in the seminar by thinking about the issues raised as they are perceived and experienced by the participants, but also as they affect you. I suggest that you have a notebook in which you record your answers. These exercises give you an invaluable opportunity to assess your life experiences to date and to determine the life you now want to create for yourself.

In Part III, 'Some singular issues', we delve a little more deeply into the practical problems that single people can experience and various ways of resolving them. Special attention is given to dilemmas that can occur because of particular circumstances. Issues that confront the single person who is a parent, or aged, or who would like to have a child, or who is homosexual, or who is single again after a relationship ends, may not be relevant to your own situation. Yet you are likely to gain further understanding of yourself and of managing life singly by considering them.

Finally, in Part IV, 'Some singular lives', several men and women who are single speak for themselves. In this series of interviews, people who are representative of various sectors of single society in terms of age, background, relationships and sexual attitudes talk about how they manage their lives.

# SOME WORDS OF THANKS

When I think about the people to whom I am grateful for making this book possible, my parents immediately come to mind; not because they have been involved in my adult single life, but because they helped instil in me much of the self-confidence that has made it possible to me to pave my own path since childhood.

I also want to thank those wonderful people such as Mary Byron, Keith Murray and George Gray who encouraged me during adolescence and early adulthood to dare to be different even though at times the road was lonely and difficult to tread.

Among the dear friends who have made me aware of the joy, support, love and understanding that can be had from friendship, I thank Rae Sinclaire, Libby Smith, Jude McBride, Pat Stewart, Ray Grose, Glenys Sharma, Garry Allen, Julie Allen, Grete and Wulf Schiefenhövel, Trevor Sinclair, Helen Davey, Ann Jackson and Deirdre and Victor Cusack.

I have also appreciated the tolerance and breathing space given me by my colleagues at Yvonne Allen and

Associates over the many months that *Successfully Single* has been in the birthing process.

I give special thanks to Val Plato, the man who has shared my life during the writing of this book.

René Gordon is my friend and publisher. She has been a spur and source of inspiration. I am delighted to have a completed manuscript and to be able to place it in her hands as a token of the confidence she has had in me.

Finally, I am grateful to all the unnamed men and women whose experiences give life and meaning to these pages and without whom *Successfully Single* would not have been written. The openness and sincerity with which they have shared the joys and dilemmas of their single lives is their gift to this book.

Yvonne Allen

First person
singular

# LET'S GET OUR BEARINGS

*S*uccessfully Single is not intended to be a song in praise of the single life, nor is it meant to be a condemnation of marriage. If you are single it is important to understand that I do not want to deter you from committing yourself now or at some future time to a partnership. Indeed, for the past ten years my consultancy has provided a way of meeting for single people who would like to have a serious relationship.

An underlying theme throughout this book is the conviction that secure, intimate friendship is necessary if our needs as human beings for warmth, recognition, touch, affection and love are to be satisfied. Only if these needs are expressed and fulfilled through intimate friendship can we extend ourselves and our potential.

So in writing about creating a successful single lifestyle I do not suggest that as a single person you 'go it alone' through life. However, the intimacy sought in marriage can also be experienced through relationships that are not limited by the marriage contract as it stands today. In fact it would seem that many a marriage is devoid of such intimacy.

You may well ask what is meant by intimate friendship?

We have an intimate relationship with someone when we can just be ourselves, when we can share our thoughts, doubts, dreams and our emotions with a friend who will accept and care for us even if they do not always agree with what we say or do. Such open and honest communication requires that we be prepared and able to take emotional risks, that we are willing to take the step of revealing our feelings and our vulnerabilities. This intimacy takes inner strength and confidence and a preparedness to learn about ourselves through sharing what we see as our weaknesses as well as our stronger points.

We have been led to believe that open, close communication comes automatically with marriage or a committed partnership, but this is not the case. Loneliness is often portrayed as a problem that plagues the life of the single person. While living singly can indeed be lonely, especially if we lack intimate friendships, some of the loneliest people are those who live in empty, non-communicative relationships. Many marriages founder because one or both partners have not had sufficient sense of their own identity to express their needs and expectations effectively and thereby develop the real closeness they seek.

Underlying this book is the conviction that unless each of us can accept and value our individuality and assert ourselves as I, first person, singular, we are unlikely to find fulfilment in our lives and our relationships.

## DO YOU HAVE A STRONG POSITIVE SENSE OF YOUR OWN IDENTITY AND WORTH AS AN INDIVIDUAL?

If you have answered 'yes' you are in a good position to live a happy and meaningful life while single. It should not be difficult for you to develop the intimacy in communication that brings a real sense of closeness and satisfaction in relationships.

However, regardless of how you see yourself now, by the time you have finished reading *Successfully Single* you will have discovered more about yourself, your life and your relationships.

## ARE YOU AT THE HELM OF YOUR JOURNEY THROUGH LIFE OR DO OTHERS CONTROL THE DIRECTIONS YOU TAKE?

From infancy onwards there are pressures upon us to follow blindly certain paths. Obviously as children we have to be dependent upon the guidance of others for our survival. However, as adults we have the ability to question the values and attitudes that have determined how we should live our lives and how worthwhile and successful we are. Each of us has the potential to take command of our own lives. We can all make conscious choices that can lead us to greater happiness.

A large proportion of the people who come to my consultancy have problems which stem from their uncritical acceptance of what they had been told from childhood about who they are and to what they should aspire. These men and women feel guilty or inadequate because they have not lived up to the expectations of family, friends, teachers, pastors, lovers or partners. They feel unhappy because they are trying to be who they should be rather than who they really are, and who they have the potential to be.

As most adults today have been brought up to believe it isn't 'right' to live singly, it is not surprising that they think there must be something wrong if they do not have a mate. The irony, which can easily be overlooked, is that there are many married people living unhappily together. If you have experienced the ending of a marriage you are likely to know, first hand, that many people who go through divorce also believe that there is something 'wrong' with them because their marriage has not turned out as it was supposed to.

It is time we examined the systems that determine 'rightness' and 'wrongness'. I encourage you to look within yourself for answers instead of dancing to the tune of what others would have you follow, even when the dance is at the expense of your own happiness.

## DO YOU WANT TO MAKE THE MOST OF YOUR UNIQUE POTENTIAL?

Of course your answer is 'yes'. As you read this book, think about how you can make the most of your life. If you find it difficult to come up with answers to the questions – don't worry. By just considering possibilities you will be setting your feet on a successful single life path.

It is likely that you will find that there are more life options available to you than you were led to believe during your adolescence. Remember that the challenges these options offer are sometimes easier to take up while you are unattached.

As we will discover, it can be difficult at times to be single. There are no clear guidelines for the person without a partner to follow. As our society is still basically geared to the family rather than to the needs of the single person, there are countless practical disadvantages. Even seemingly small things like having to pay twice the price for the contents of small rather than family-sized packages of perishables or having to pay supplements for single rooms when travelling can be irritating.

There are practical obstacles to living singly, but many of the problems are manufactured more by conditioning than by reality. With a change in attitude, what has constituted a negative experience, like dining in a restaurant or going overseas alone, can be converted into an enjoyable challenge.

No matter whether you are without a partner through choice or circumstance, something to always bear in mind is that being a single person does not mean being alone. There are plenty of men and women who are potentially available if we are prepared to initiate contact and offer the gift of friendship.

## Some single stereotypes

According to the dictionary 'single' means 'unmarried'. In itself this definition seems relatively harmless. Yet, in reality it is laden with values that imply that to be married is the normal state, an assumption that can impose restrictions on the happiness of the single person.

WHAT DOES THE WORD 'SINGLE' MEAN TO YOU?

Are the images that come to your mind positive or negative? Why?

As we shall see age, sex, education, material standard of living, occupation and individual physical and personality characteristics do influence the likelihood of our being partnered. However, the label 'single' encompasses people from age 16 to over 100, from all socioeconomic levels, from all religious and political persuasions and educational and family backgrounds.

Today an increasing number of those who are single have previously been married or coupled. Yet because of the commonly held stereotypes, the label 'single' can make them feel uncomfortable even though they are no longer with their partner. Many who are once again 'unmarried' would prefer to be deemed divorced or separated despite the negative connotations these labels can also bring.

At the outset I caution you to be aware of the limitations of labelling yourself. It is important to realise that you are very much what you define yourself to be. If you regard being without a partner as negative it is likely that your self-image as a single and your attitude to your life are also unnecessarily negative.

There are as many different experiences of being single and living life without a partner as there are single people. Recognising this, the term 'single' in this book will simply signify an adult person who is not committed to a particular relationship or partner, be this through choice or circumstance. While census statistics on marital status are quoted through these pages, it is interesting to note that unknown numbers of those deemed single would regard themselves as in a partnership.

## Singularly odd?

If we look at the known history of Western civilisation we can see that the adult man or woman who has lived life without a partner has often been depicted as eccentric, as unfortunate, or as homosexual (and therefore as eccentric or unfortunate), or as a person with a religious or an ideological vocation that demands single-minded commitment. During the Middle Ages it was not uncommon for women who were single to be seen as evil and burnt at the stake as witches.

No longer do these damaging stereotypes make sense to us. In the United States in 1981 it was estimated that approximately one in every three people between the ages of 20 and 55 – about 50 million adults – were single (J. Simenauer and D. Carroll *Singles: The New Americans*). In 1984 more than three in ten Australians over 21 were living without a partner. Surely these figures reflect too substantial a sector of a population for it to be deemed peculiar or in quest of a monastic mission. It is unreasonable to assume that such a large number of people live unfortunate and unhappy lives while unattached.

Indeed, in recent times there has been a swing away from depicting the person without a partner as unfortunate. Marketing people have realised the buying power of the single person's dollar and it is now often portrayed as trendy rather than odd to be alone. Yet, the glamorous and hedonistic pictures painted of a single lifestyle can be as damaging to self-image and confidence as the negative stereotypes of spinster and mummy's boy that once plagued the person alone.

# WHY SAIL LIFE SOLO?

*C*ensus figures for the last decade show marked changes in the profile of the populations in Western countries in terms of age, marital status and the composition of families and households. These changes reflect a shift away from the traditional nuclear family which comprised a couple and their dependent children.

In Australia in 1981, just over one in three households varied from the traditional family unit founded on the couple. A major factor influencing this move has been the dramatic increase in the incidence of divorce.

Australia is not alone in experiencing a tremendous increase in the rate of divorce which almost tripled between 1971 and 1981. Similar increases occurred in several other Western countries including the United States, Britain, Sweden and France.

This growing tendency of couples to terminate marriage means that many men and women will experience living as a single again, at least once during their adult lifetime, be this through their own choice or the decision of their partner. While living singly these people establish households that vary from the family unit to which they had become accustomed. These days it is not uncommon to find a number of unrelated adults sharing a home base for convenience and companionship.

For a lot of people being single is a time between being partnered. This phase is important not only because there are particular challenges that confront the person who is single again, but also because it provides these people with a tremendous opportunity to stop and take stock of their lives and their relationship needs.

Given the high rate of marriage failure, it is not surprising that a large number of once-marrieds now head households as single parents. The increased preparedness for unmarried mothers to keep and raise their children has also added to the number of households where only one parent is present.

# Single by choice

More than ever before we have, as adults, a tremendous range of life options. Many people are now choosing to live without partners. For some, this may be a short-term arrangement while exploring being independent and autonomous. For others it is for a lifetime.

There has been a marked change in the age at which men and women marry for the first time. The most popular age for first marriages in 1981 was between 25 and 29 for men and between 20 and 24 years for women. And more than 35 per cent of women married for the first time in their late twenties.

The majority of people I see who are partner-seeking are between 30 and 40 years old and, of these, approximately 40 per cent have never been married. Often the reason they give for having remained single is choice rather than circumstance.

They had decided to establish their careers and a secure life before settling down. While they may have had significant relationships, these men and women chose to have a time of personal consolidation before committing themselves to a partnership and a family.

Today it is not unusual to meet single people who have no intention of ever being married. A survey of three thousand singles in the United States in 1981 revealed that 25 per cent of those responding were not interested in marrying or having a particular partner (J. Simenauer and D. Carroll *Singles: The New Americans*). As we shall see, women who are revelling in the freedom and independence that women's liberation has brought them, number among those who show little interest in marriage. Eight per cent of never-married women in Melbourne who responded to a questionnaire about living singly conducted by Penman and Stolk and reported in their interesting book *Not the Marrying Kind*, stated that they had no wish to marry, and 22.5 per cent said that they found being single entirely satisfying.

Presumably, a large number of these dedicated singles appreciate the benefits of living without a mate. Some of these advantages will be discussed in Part Four when I interview people who are happily single by choice. Their lives demonstrate that there are viable and satisfying alternatives to being in a committed relationship.

## Single because I'm scared

On the other hand, many people choose to be single not because they enjoy living solo, but because they fear the consequences of involvement and commitment. Often they have learned about their vulnerability through the knocks of the hard school of experience and their anxiety is understandable.

Yet, just as a fear of being single is a dangerous motive for marrying, so, too, a fear of having a close relationship is a negative and growth-stunting approach to life. While our lives are bounded by fear and mistrust it is unlikely we will realise our potential for happiness be we single or otherwise.

DO YOU FEAR BEING EMOTIONALLY CLOSE TO ANYONE?

If so, I hope that reading this book will help you to realise the advantages of friendship, regardless of whether or not you want the risk of a committed partnership or marriage. I believe that whether you are 18, 33, 46, 60 or 95 years old, intimate companionship is the source of the deepest satisfaction most of us can experience as human beings.

## The gay option

The increased size of the single population is due also to the growing preparedness of homosexuals to declare their sexual preferences and eschew the norm of heterosexual marriages. In Part III I examine some of the particular difficulties that are associated with the gay single lifestyle. However, whether they are in committed relationships or not, men and women who are homosexual have similar needs for intimate friendships as do heterosexuals and many of the issues discussed through these pages are equally relevant to them as to the person who is 'straight'.

# Single through circumstance

Some people who are single do believe themselves to be unfortunate. They regard their not having a partner as a result of circumstance. The reasons for their being alone could be any one of the following.

## On the lookout but not looked for

For many people, living without a partner is assumed to be a temporary phase prior to their having a significant relationship or marrying. Some appreciate the independence this phase offers while others regard themselves as unlucky and as biding their time until someone special comes into their lives. While a hoped-for partner probably will appear, this 'treading water' approach can restrict their individual development and happiness.

At a recent seminar I conducted on 'Making More of a Single Lifestyle', a man in his early thirties said he longed for a partner so that he could 'really start living'. I pointed out to him that it is vital that we get on with living our lives, maximising the experience of the present. We can still have an interesting and enjoyable life now even if we desire to share with someone special in the future. While single we can also become aware of what we would like to find in a partner and a relationship from the other people we date and mix with socially.

However, the reality is that the chances of finding a partner are not equal for everyone. . .

## Are the odds in your favour?

If we look at the marriage gradient we can see that in fact the odds are stacked against many men and women who would like to be partnered, because of their sex, age, socioeconomic background, physical appearance, personality, education, occupation and their expectations of a relationship and a mate. While some people have always been disadvantaged in their quest of a mate, changes in the population profile and in expectations held of a relationship have made it difficult for many very eligible people to find a compatible partner.

For the first time in Australia, women outnumber men in terms of the total adult population. It has recently been estimated that there is currently a surplus of 129 568 women aged 16 plus. Put another way, for every 100 female adults over 15 years of age there are 97 males (The Bulletin, 21 May 1985).

Penman and Stolk in Not the Marrying Kind estimate that by the age of 50, almost 50 per cent of Australian women live without a partner. If they wish to find a mate their chances are limited. Females start to outnumber males from the age of 55 plus. By age 75 there are almost twice as many women as there are men.

Older women today outnumber men because they tend to live longer and because many males were killed during the Second World War. Although single women in these age groups are not necessarily partner-seeking, the implications that this shortage of males in these groups holds for women are important. Regardless of their marital status, it is inevitable that the majority of women will be alone in the later years of life.

# A male shortage

The 1981 census shows that males still outnumber females in all age groups between 16 and 55. However, as far as partner-seeking is concerned, there is an imbalance of available partners because of the traditional expectations that men and women hold about the age of an ideal mate.

According to Bettina Arndt, well-known sex therapist and consultant, it would seem that women in Australia are creating a partner shortage for themselves because they tend to look for men who are more mature than they are. She has estimated that Australian women seek a mate who is two years older than themselves — and there aren't enough of them to go round (The *Bulletin*, 21 May 1985).

However, according to my experience with people who are partner-seeking, women are more flexible than men about age. Most men express a strong preference for younger women. I have found that men are usually very reluctant to meet a woman who is any older than they are and that they often state a definite preference to meet someone who is considerably younger. While 95 per cent of my female clients are willing, many even keen, to meet men who are their junior, only 5 per cent of males are prepared to explore the delights of the older woman.

# The marriage squeeze

It is this preference by men for younger women rather than women wanting older men that has caused what is now referred to as 'the marriage squeeze'. However, while men continue to partner women who are younger than themselves, whether this be through their own preference or that of the female, statistically there will be fewer of them available to each group of women who are in search of a mate.

Brian English, a family researcher at the University of New South Wales, has estimated that in Australia by 1990, women who are 35 and partner-seeking will be in 'the tightest market situation this century'. He estimates that if women continue to partner with men two years older than themselves, there will only be 65 available men for every 100 women by the year 2000 (The *Bulletin*, 21 May 1985).

# No one in sight for the fair and bright

Bettina Arndt's investigations (The *Bulletin*, 21 May 1985) and my own professional experience lead to the conclusion that the shortage of men does not affect all women equally. The chances of finding a partner are actually worst for those women who are considered to be the best and brightest. Given the conditioning that a woman should marry a man who is better educated, more successful and so on, than herself, then the more a woman achieves, the less likely it is that she will find a suitable mate.

Evidence of the difficulty attractive, intelligent, successful women can have in meeting 'superior' males can be seen in the phenomenon of advertisements lodged in highly regarded newspapers in which women seek out potentially suitable men.

## Some men are also disadvantaged

It is apparent from the marriage gradient that just as single women who find it hard to meet partners are likely to be successful and in professional or management occupations, single men who have had low levels of education and have been unemployed or in low status jobs are likely to be disadvantaged. They are the men few women regard as better than themselves and therefore they are undesirable as marriage partners.

These men 'at the bottom' are far more disadvantaged than the women 'at the top'. As I will discuss later, women are better equipped to live singly than males as long as their needs for economic survival are met. One of the reasons why the successful woman can find herself single through circumstance is because she is not prepared to compromise her choice of a partner. But, the man who seemingly has little to offer, has few, if any, opportunities for compromise even if he so wanted.

## Single but a package

Those who are single through the circumstance of a relationship ending, no longer experience the stigma that once reduced significantly their chances of meeting a potential mate. Divorce is the norm rather than the exception these days. However the likelihood of someone who is single again finding another partner is not only dependent, as we have seen, on the availability of potential mates which varies according to their sex, age and their socioeconomic status but also on whether or not they have children.

Men and women who are single parents can find their opportunities for meeting potential mates seriously restricted. As we will discuss at length later, the responsibilities of caring for children leave little opportunity for socialising, and having a ready-made family does not appeal to many of the unattached who are wanting to find a partner.

## Judging a book by its cover

Apart from the variables so far mentioned, physical and personality factors can also restrict the opportunities a person has to meet a mate. While some singles believe they are less desirable because of their particular appearance or temperament, this does not mean that there is not someone who would be appreciative of them, especially if they develop their own unique potentialities.

A friend of mine once said to me 'for every Mr Hippo, there is a Mrs Hippo somewhere'. While this may be so, anyone who does not fit into the current image of physical attractiveness is at a disadvantage in our society. The emphasis placed on physical fitness today makes excess fat undesirable to the majority of partner-seekers: to look like a magazine model is the supposed ideal. Similarly to be very short and male or toweringly tall and female can reduce the chances of meeting a mate, especially if one is self-conscious about being different.

Many relationships fail to last because of the undue emphasis placed on physical attraction. Unfortunately, when selecting a partner, appearance all too often outweighs other important factors – such as shared attitudes and values – which are far more likely to determine the success of a relationship.

While seemingly superficial, it is a reality that people do tend to make judgments about each other on the basis of appearance before anything else. When meeting for the first time, we often have little else to go by. Therefore it is up to us to make the most of ourselves, if for no other reason than to reflect our own self-esteem. How we present can say a great deal about how we value ourselves.

# MARRIAGE ... AN INSECURE MOORING?

hy do the majority of us still opt to marry when nearly 40 per cent of marriages today end in divorce? While the odds are so stacked against the survival of marriage it does seem a risky if not masochistic step. Those who are confirmed singles by choice could well argue that they do not intend racing towards wedlock like lemmings over a precipice only to land in a marriage on the rocks.

In Australia and the United States, marriage has not gone out of fashion even though there is an increasing number of couples who are choosing to live in de facto relationships or are putting off marriage indefinitely. Unlike Sweden, Norway, France and Britain where the number of couples marrying has decreased since 1970, the number of marriages taking place in Australia each year is on the increase, after having fluctuated downwards quite substantially during the decade 1970–80. An examination of the statistics reveals that whereas in 1971 approximately two in ten of those marrying were doing so for the second or more time; in 1984, almost 50 per cent of those marrying had been previously divorced or widowed.

To me these figures suggest that rather than marriage becoming increasingly popular, there are those who see themselves as 'the marrying kind', people who are willing to venture down the aisle again and again, if needs be, in quest of what they believe marriage has to offer them.

It does not seem to be solely the lure of promised joy that leads couples to the altar. On the contrary, in Ailsa Burns' Sydney survey the majority of those interviewed said that they had known on their wedding day that they should not be taking this step. Even before making their vows they had realised their marriage had little hope of working. Yet they still went ahead (A. Burns *Breaking Up; Marriage and Separation in Australia*).

Among the reasons such seemingly doomed couples give for marrying are not wanting to hurt their partner, a preparedness to do what their parents and friends expected, a desire not to live alone, wanting to break free of their parental home and a need to feel their future was secure. Not one of these reasons reflects the positive desire of the individual to be with their mate; each reason is in response to some outside pressure. Small wonder so many marriages are doomed to failure.

## What's gone wrong with marriage?

I believe the long-held view of human partnership is in need of debate and change. The time has come for us to ask what it is we really want and need from our friendships and, more particularly, potential partnerships and marriage. My professional experience leads me to conclude that most of us have not been encouraged to pose such questions. Yet if we want to find happiness we must ask ourselves:

WHAT DO RELATIONSHIPS MEAN TO ME?

Too many people who tread the marriage path, especially those who do so repeatedly, make the mistake of not seriously asking themselves:

WHAT AM I LOOKING FOR IN A PARTNER?

WHAT DO I EXPECT FROM A MARRIAGE?

HOW MUCH DOES THE FEAR OF BEING SINGLE PRESSURE
ME INTO RELATIONSHIPS?

## The baby boom generation

The sixties witnessed the emergence of philosophies associated with the human potential movement. These philosophies have particularly influenced the generation born after the Second World War — the baby boom generation. Rather than emphasising the welfare of the family, the community and society as a whole, these philosophies focused more on the development of the individual. As a result, it is no longer considered selfish to want to maximise your own talents.

If we want to explore, expand and express our unique potentialities, marriage as we know it can be a stultifying prison. Most of us do not have to look far beyond our own relationships and those of our family and friends to see examples of how individuality can all too readily be exchanged for the illusory bliss of coupledom.

Perhaps because I am one of the baby boom generation, I want to encourage you to explore and value your individuality. If you are to manage your life effectively it is important for you to develop self-awareness and an understanding of your relationship needs. The responsibility for your happiness rests largely on your own shoulders and the way to achieve happiness is to devise strategies by which you can be better prepared and equipped to live as an autonomous individual. Only if you are able to lead a satisfying life as a single will you be able to commit yourself to a partnership or marriage founded on a solid and enduring basis of mutual and mature interdependence, rather than on a dependence bred out of insecurity.

## Who am I without a partner?

Often when a relationship comes to an end there is an identity crisis for one or both partners who, by being a couple, have lost – or avoided – their true selves.

Many marriages begin breaking down when one of the partners starts to express their individual needs — be this by further study, moving house to pursue career advancement or, especially for women, finding a job that satisfies a need to achieve — and the other cannot adjust to, or accept, this change. The distress and divorce that often results could well have been prevented. The marriage contract needed today should encourage both partners to foster their development as individuals as well as their development as a couple. Two people entering a partnership should contract to communicate their individual needs, desires, doubts and expectations to each other from the start. Recognising and voicing their individuality at the outset is the way towards developing intimacy, keeping their relationship alive and increasing its chances of lasting.

For the partnered reader, ask yourself:

WHO AM I WITHOUT MY PARTNER?

Don't ever forget that having a strong sense of your identity could prove to be an invaluable insurance policy in the event of anything happening to your relationship.

# A different agenda

The contract that has been the foundation of marriage for centuries once served its purpose. To pledge 'to love, honour and obey until death us do part' made sense when to marry was to enter a mutually advantageous partnership founded on needs for economic security and the propagation and protection of children. Although it did little to foster the idea of individuality, this contract had relevance when women were housewives and men the breadwinners.

Until women were needed in the workforce – during the Second World War in Australia – the marriage contract formalised an exchange of services. In return for the husband providing his wife material security, she would give him the nurturing support that he had received from his mother. Both would be able to express their sexual drives safely and the offspring that resulted from their intercourse would be legitimised by their marriage. Apparent sexual exclusivity was a price both were expected to pay for the stability and the security that their relationship was meant to give them and their children. This provided the ground rules for their social and economic unit to operate, if not always happily. However, no longer do economic and sexual motives explain why we marry.

## Economic independence

These days most single men and women who have employment are quite capable of satisfying their survival needs and more. No longer does a single woman need to exchange her individuality and freedom for the material security which only marriage previously made possible.

## Sexual freedom

No longer do we need to marry to have our sexual needs met. The development of effective contraception has made it possible to have sexual relationships without risk of producing unwanted children. And the irrelevance of the marriage contract has resulted in individuals and couples consciously choosing to have children out of wedlock.

Without a marriage partner we cannot assume that there is someone available to satisfy our sexual needs. At the same time, however, we are not bound to have sex out of a sense of duty as ordained by our marriage vow. Women do not have to trade their bodies in order to have a roof over their heads and men can make sexual advances without it being a statement of marital intent.

# You and me against the world

Unrealistic as it may seem, given the short life-expectancy of many marriages, a major force underlying the popularity of marriage is a desire to find security, stability and a sense of belonging in an increasingly insecure and unstable world.

The quest for security and stability is understandable, for I believe it to be a basic need each of us has whether we marry or not. To cope alone with the pressures of life in the 1980s is not easy. That we seek solace and support through partnering makes sense. With few exceptions, all of us are aware of the comfort and support congenial company can give us in times of trouble.

Many of us feel insignificant, but a cog in a wheel, unable to influence the world around us. Also, more than at any time in our history we are party to the problems of people unknown to us in the world at large. Advances in communications technology have made us members of a global village. Yet, they have also brought the incredible tragedy, misery and suffering of people from the four corners of the earth into our very homes, adding to our tensions.

As well as seemingly reducing our world and alerting us to the plight of people whose circumstances we can do nothing about, the media can at the same time isolate us. When so much of our life is lived in front of these impersonal means of communications we are likely to know more about the deprivations of a rebel in Afghanistan than we are of the worries of our next door neighbour.

We seek companionship to counter this stress; indeed warm, supportive relationships are a vital ingredient in the recipe I recommend to help to lighten the load.

Ideally, a partnership creates a shared haven in which we can give and receive warmth and recognition that helps us to feel significant and valued. So it is no wonder that marriage for many is seen as a means of ensuring companionship through good times and bad. For some this does happen, yet for others, instead of providing a buffer against the pressures of the world, marriage can be the source of devastating tension that only adds to the problems of living.

Given the obvious advantages that having a committed relationship and sharing life's pressures can provide:

## WHY DO SO MANY MARRIAGES FAIL TO PROVIDE THE SECURITY AND STABILITY PROMISED?

Considering research findings in Australia and overseas, I cannot help but conclude that the institution of marriage does not meet our needs in the 1980s because:

- The picture painted of coupledom is often unrealistic and leads to expectations of a partner and marriage that cannot be met;
- The traditional guidelines we have had for marriage have not prepared us adequately for the intimate sharing

required if the relationship is to grow and be fulfilling;

- And so, intimate friendship is lacking in many, if not the majority, of marriages;
- The contract is inappropriate to meet the needs both partners have for individual development, and therefore
- For many of us, especially for women who want to be more than housewives, marriage as we have known it has proved to be a prison.

# SIGHTS SET ON COUPLEDOM ... DIFFERENT SEX, DIFFERENT ISSUES

Despite the dramatic changes in technology and lifestyle of this century, most of us have been brought up to assume that we would become one of a couple. The sources of authority in our lives be they parents, teachers, politicians, priests or our peer group have encouraged partnering.

Most of us have lived in a family where there was a mother, a father and at least one brother or sister. We took it for granted that this was how life was meant to be. We learned what was expected of us as a son or daughter and our parents were models for what we would be like when we were grown up.

## What should little boys be made of and become?

Most men who are adults in the 1980s were taught from childhood to repress their soft, sensitive sides. As boys they were taught to be strong, aggressive and competitive.

They were encouraged to get ahead in life so that they could find a good job and earn a secure income. The more they attained in the material sense, the more desirable and successful they would be as a husband and father.

It is still assumed today that doing well at school and sport assures a man's way into the best jobs and the best marriages. A husband knows that his part of the marriage contract is his duty to provide for, and to protect, those in his care. It is assumed that happiness will automatically follow. Unfortunately men who have been reared in this way are given little idea of how to establish and develop a relationship that is likely to satisfy both partners throughout their life together.

Given the willingness with which women are leaving even successful and wealthy partners these days, we can only conclude that what has been perceived as desirable for a male to achieve and possess does not necessarily add up to happiness or success in marriage. No wonder so many men say that they just don't know what women really want of them or of a relationship.

## ... and what about little girls?

Until the last decade or so, girls from childhood onwards were also prepared for their 'natural' destiny of marriage. Most females who are adults today were taught as young-sters to aim at 'snaring' a desirable man who could look after them well. They were encouraged to find a partner superior to themselves in achievement, earning ability and maturity.

To attract a desirable mate they learned that they should be pretty and pleasing. As adolescents it was to their advantage to strive to be as physically attractive as the latest fashions and cosmetics allowed. They believed that 'plain Janes' and girls with brains would be left behind in the marriage stakes.

From an early age they knew it was important to learn how to look after a man and a home. To be a 'good catch' they had to have the nurturing and home-making skills that the breadwinner would want at the end of his hard-working day. While schooling for both sexes has been compulsory for many years, in the past education for the majority of girls seems to have been more to show levels of accomplishment than to pave the way to successful careers.

Today it is generally accepted – and indeed by many people expected – that a woman will work to help support her family. Yet, as the marriage gradient indicates, doing well at school and succeeding in a career can be a definite disadvantage for the single woman seeking a partner. Given the conditioning that the adult males and females of today typically had as children, it is not surprising that a woman's beauty and domestic prowess are still more highly prized than her brains and achievement by many men. It is also no wonder that a woman herself often finds it difficult to value her own abilities and achievements.

# Man, singular

In coming to terms with the challenges of living without a partner, different issues confront us depending on whether we have been brought up as males or females. This child raising, based on gender, has had a tremendous influence on what we have come to expect in our relationships as adult men and women. It affects how we experience living as a single.

One of the myths associated with the label 'single' is that it is preferable to be male and fancy free than to be a woman without a partner. Yet several studies have shown that despite the image of the free-wheeling bachelor and the unfortunate spinster, to be unattached is a healthier and happier state for women than it is for men. Evidence strongly suggests that the single woman is not only far less prone to physical and psychological problems than her male counterpart, but is also likely to be sounder of body and mind than women who have married (S. Mugford and J. Lally *Australian Journal of Social Issues*).

On the other hand, married men have been shown to be less likely to have physical and psychological problems than bachelors. Males who are single after having experienced the ending of a marriage through death or divorce appear to be at the highest level of risk (J. Bernard *The Future of Marriage*).

A recent report by Peter Jordan *The Effects of Marital*

*Separation on Men 'Men Hurt'* issued by the Family Court of Australia supported these conclusions showing that, generally speaking, it was far more devastating for men than women to experience being on their own after separation and divorce. Husbands were far more prone to suffering health problems and emotional distress when adjusting to living alone than were their wives. Bearing this in mind, it is not surprising to find that after divorce men are far more likely than women to remarry and do so in a shorter space of time.

When marriages break up, big strong men are frequently surprised to find themselves totally at a loss and acting like infants. Counsellor Peter Jordan who presented his research findings to the Family Court of Australia reported that males involved in separation proceedings were often frightened by the depth of their distress. Men interviewed would describe themselves as 'breaking down', as if they were machines. It seems that when most men show emotion they believe that they are at risk of falling apart, and this causes them tremendous anxiety. The anger, rage or helplessness that colours their reaction may seem immature, yet it is surely an understandable response. For some men it is as if 'the breast' has been taken away.

## In quest of a breast

Although supposedly the stronger and more independent sex, most males have not been reared to look after themselves effectively, especially at an emotional level. To be partnered is a way a man can seek to ensure that the fulfilment he first found at his mother's breast, and then took for granted during his developing years, continues into manhood. For many a man, his wife or lover takes on the mothering role of tending to his needs for love, support, comfort and caring. She also attends to the practical day to day concerns of his home so that he can go out to meet the demands and challenges of his world, secure of mind, heart and body.

Given the satisfactions and security of this home base, it is no wonder that living without a partner can be so much harder for men, especially if they have previously been married or in a committed relationship. It is also not difficult to understand why so many males cannot accept the changing role of women, and the equality that they are now demanding in relationships. Their mothers taught them to expect something quite different!

If you are a man who has recently been through a separation or a divorce, don't think there is anything wrong with you if you are finding yourself overwhelmed by emotions at times and if you are feeling totally at a loss when you are on your own. It is quite normal and healthy for you to feel this way.

Many separated and divorced men acknowledge that they avoid facing up to the problems of being alone. Some escape through alcohol and male company. Unfortunately in most instances such company would seem to lack the intimate open communication they really need. It helps them to forget rather than work through their feelings of distress, rejection, anger and hopelessness.

Often men who are unhappily single say that they frequent bars or clubs or discos no matter how unsatisfactory they find such places to be. They may see it as a weakness, but they simply cannot do without the feelings of security that being with a woman or women give them.

It is common practice for many a man to seek solace through one-night stands after the break-up of a relationship. It is easy to assume that these encounters are based on their desire for sexual contact. Sex is supposed to be what drives a man into a woman's arms. However this needs questioning. After talking with such casanovas I find time and time again that underlying the bed-hopping syndrome is a desire for the deeper feelings of security and comfort that an embrace can give — and an urgent need not to be overwhelmed by the fear of being alone.

Because of their conditioning, men also seem more prepared than women to have a far from ideal partnership rather than none at all. The majority of them seem to require a relationship – even an unsatisfactory one – from which to go out into the world, if they are to live up to the image of the independent, achieving male.

Traditionally, husbands have achieved satisfaction in their lives outside the home, and have had more ready access to other sexual partners than their wives. They have been in a better position to turn a blind eye to the unsatisfactory aspects of their marriage than women whose satisfaction in life has largely hinged on the adequacy of their partnership. Therefore, when a man initiates a separation it is likely to be because he has met another woman, and found another base from which to go out into the world, rather than because he is merely dissatisfied with his marriage.

## The recycled male

Despite the commonly held view that it is easier for men to go out and socialise than it is for women, many a man is left socially isolated when a relationship comes to an end. The 'how tos' of starting again can be just as unclear and difficult for both sexes.

It is not uncommon for me to hear an accomplished businessman just out of a long-term marriage say he is totally at a loss as to how to go about mixing with women and dating again. Whether to ask someone in for coffee or 'to take a look at his etchings' can cause more anxiety than most boardroom decisions.

Unfortunately, many of the avenues for meeting pressure men and women into playing traditional games. All too often their communication is based on role playing and is superficial. The atmosphere brings out much that is competitive, leaving little opportunity for them really to relate, despite their underlying desire to share.

Many men do not seem to acquire the social skills that women have learned about fostering and looking after relationships. Most men seem to know more about mateship than deep friendship with other men and have little understanding of how to talk intimately with a woman. Their traditional conditioning is exposed when they regard women more as potential conquests or sex partners than as friends, and fellow males as potential rivals – both at work and on the personal level – than as intimates. No wonder it can be difficult for men to express their emotions.

## Look to the woman within

To live successfully as a single man you must recognise, express and satisfy the more feminine aspects of your nature. The cut and thrust of competitive sport, business and relationships, the acquiring of material symbols of success and the challenge of controlling nature through science and technology offer abundant opportunities to engage and satisfy your masculine side. Yet it is likely that you have been deprived of the right to know, understand and express your emotions, your intuition, your sensitivity, your ability to nurture and your need to find deeper, spiritual meanings in life – the feminine elements of yourself that are not linked to external achievements.

## Learn from living singly

At the practical level, living singly equips you with domestic skills. Learning to look after yourself assists you to see yourself outside the conventional male roles and to realise that you do not need a partner 'to do' for you. The lack of a partner is also likely to make you more aware of the needs you have for touch, warmth, companionship, love and affection – all of which you may have taken for granted as being provided by the women in your life, be they mother, lover or wife. I believe that living alone offers you a rare opportunity to bring together your masculine abilities and your feminine aspects; and in integrating these two aspects find a sense of wholeness.

If you can ignore the lures that the image-makers put to you about the trappings the successful single needs, you can determine the life values that are important to you and live by them. You can change career, explore your creativity, drop out of the rat race or whatever, without risking the security of others.

As long as men are repressed by the image of what it is to be 'a man' and while women strive to cater to their needs, men will have limited access to the richness of their whole selves and sadly for women, their ability to give the nurturance that women also need.

# Woman, singular

Why are single women likely to be healthier and happier than married women or single males?

It may seem strange that women appear to need men less than men need them. We only have to compare magazines for women with those written for men to see how much more females are seen to focus their attention on relationships than do males. It is commonly assumed that a man is meant to be everything in a woman's life while a woman is but a part of a man's. Yet the fact is that men, from childhood on, are dependent on females for much of their well-being.

No one questions that in the womb and at birth male and female infants alike have similar needs. For the first months they are nourished and nurtured in the same way. It is vital that as infants they be fed, touched, cared for, and have a stimulating environment if they are to be physically and mentally healthy.

Similarly, as adults, women and men both have strong needs for being nourished emotionally and psychologically. However, for most women, their upbringing has taught them to satisfy their own needs indirectly by looking after those of others. Often their own feelings of satisfaction are dependent on the happiness of others.

Marriage gives a woman ample opportunity to exercise her nurturing skills as she tends to the needs of her partner and offspring. However, unless her partner is in tune with his feelings and able to express them and is concerned to satisfy her needs, it is unlikely that her innate requirements will be fulfilled. Unfortunately, as we have seen, men have not usually been brought up with a strong awareness of their capacity to nurture a partner.

Marriage as a rule has not encouraged the expression of the woman's masculine qualities. Traditionally, any impact she has had upon the world beyond her home has been second-hand, expressed through her partner or her children rather than through her individually recognised effort.

Even if she has a job or makes use of a talent, a married woman is still more apt to identify herself by her relationship to her partner and family than by her career or abilities. She is 'John's wife' and 'Joanne's mother' before she is a schoolteacher or an artist.

As long as meeting the needs of her man and children are a woman's prime concern it can be extremely difficult if not impossible for her to assert her own needs, express her abilities or explore her potentiality outside her roles of wife and mother. Even in this age of women's liberation it is understandable that married women experience the very real conflicts that prompt so many of them to seek medical assistance and counselling. Often it is a matter of a loss of identity. It is not surprising, therefore, that research has revealed marriage to be not as happy a solution to life ever after for women as it is for men.

## How can a woman become herself?

One way is through learning to live effectively as a single – be this until she has a strong sense of herself, her needs and her potentialities, or be this for a lifetime.

As might be expected today, just as single men have to come to terms with their so-called feminine qualities, similarly, the woman who lives singly faces the challenge of developing her masculine aspects. Unfortunately many women marry before they have had any real opportunity to develop this part of themselves.

Until recent years, a woman who lived independently of a man was often stereotyped as masculine, as a 'ball breaker' and as undesirable. I can readily recall the maiden aunts and unmarried school ma'ams who strode across the pages of schoolgirl novels. By portraying these women as asexual and not attractive in a feminine sense it was suggested that they were born with an oversupply of male genes or a lack of the sugar and spice that makes women so nice.

Although dramatic changes have taken place which have liberated single women from such restrictive images, those who live without a man are sometimes still depicted as being masculine, butch or unattractive. Yet many of the women who are proud to be single today are undeniably desirable to men. They flaunt their feminine appeal in the face of long-held negative stereotypes as they pursue lifestyles that express such 'masculine' traits as ambition and independence.

Some choose to live their lives without having a sexual relationship with a man. Whether they live alone or in lesbian relationships, they prefer to be free of a sexual dependence on men. For some this choice is a political one, a statement against the male attitudes and values that have oppressed women throughout history. Many of them have in fact been married or have had male lovers which puts paid to the myth that a woman is alone or lesbian because she can't get a man.

## A good man can be hard to find

As we have seen, because of an imbalance in sex ratios and changing expectations of relationships, there is indeed a shortage of men for many women who would like to be partnered. But it is not only the lack of available men that makes more and more women over 30 choose not to have relationships with men; they do so because they are unable to meet the sort of man they would like to have as a partner. They are very selective and prefer not to compromise. Even though their sexual needs are not being met, they would nevertheless prefer to be on their own than 'make do'.

Of the single women over 30 who responded to a recent survey of 1000 Australian women between 18 and 40 conducted for *Cleo* magazine (March 1985), 65 per cent said that the men who were available weren't worth the effort of finding and 33 per cent said that they had given up looking and chose to be celibate.

There is no doubt that it can be very difficult for a woman who is not interested in having casual affairs to meet a compatible mate, so it is not surprising that celibacy is seen by many sexually inactive women as due to circumstance rather than to desire. However, a growing number of women who are single do profess to be celibate by choice. Eleven per cent of all of the women surveyed by *Cleo* said that they have no interest in having a sexual relationship. For some this decision will be short-term, for others it could well be for a lifetime.

In the Penman and Stolk survey (*Not the Marrying*

*Kind*) of single women in Melbourne, nearly half of the respondents said they had not had any sexual activity ranging from kissing to intercourse for at least six months and only one in every six indicated 'regularly' as their response. Yet 89 per cent of all the women surveyed said they were satisfied with being single, even if two out of three were open to change if a suitable partner came into their life.

## Superwoman?

A dilemma many women who enjoy being single find difficult to resolve is how to hold on to the gains that have been won with the advent of women's liberation and have a partnership with a man at the same time. While there are obviously some who manage to be superwoman – juggling being wife, mother, lover, domestic, businesswoman and companion simultaneously – even for the most adept at switching and combining roles, the going can be tough.

Rather than trying to meet the needs and expectations of a mate as well as pursuing a demanding career, a number of women are choosing to stay single while enjoying male relationships without commitment. If they opt for an independent lifestyle this does not necessarily mean that they are celibate or gay. The majority of single respondents to both *Cleo* and Penman and Stolk surveys were interested in having an active sex life and had no intention of a life devoid of male company.

## Can a woman be happy without a mate?

Although a generalisation, I think it fair to say that women do not need to be dependent on men for the satisfaction of most of their emotional and sensual requirements. Throughout history many of their needs for warmth, touch, affection and intimacy have been satisfied through their relationships with their families and, very importantly, through their sharing with other women.

While traditionally they have been conditioned to repress their more aggressive and assertive masculine attributes, women have not been expected to cut off their emotions and feelings in the way men have. It is quite acceptable for them to hug and kiss each other, to share their disappointments and their experiences — to be intimate with each other — whereas for a man to do so may be seen as a sign of weakness or of his being homosexual.

So, women who are single are not necessarily emotionally deprived. The issues they face living solo are more to do with overcoming their conditioning, asserting themselves beyond domesticity, and to unabashedly obtaining satisfaction directly from their own actions and achievements.

First and foremost, women who live without a partner must learn to be economically independent and manage their material affairs. Yet, achieving in what was once a man's domain and learning not to be afraid of success can be difficult for women who have been taught that it is not ladylike to be ambitious and competitive.

How effectively you handle being single as a woman is influenced by your age, education, and relationship experience, as well as your expectations and conditioning. It is far easier, for example, if you have always been single to develop the masculine attributes within yourself than it is if you are used to having a partner. But for the woman who finds herself 'single again', the battle for survival can be quite daunting.

Despite the difficulties that frequently face a woman who is single again, especially if she has children, one of the changes that has accompanied the liberation of women has been the increased incidence of women initiating separation and divorce. The 1985 Family Court of Australia report (Peter Jordan *The Effects of Marital Separation on Men 'Men Hurt'*) revealed that in 65 per cent of the cases studied, the wife was the one to make the decision to separate, whereas the husband's decision accounted for only 19 per cent of divorces. Only in 16 per cent of cases was the divorce the result of mutual agreement.

## Supermum

While women who have had a partnership seem to adjust more easily to living alone than do men, especially if they were the ones to initiate the separation, it can be difficult for them to cope with the practical problems associated with maintaining themselves and their families if they have children.

Single mothers with children in their custody constitute the largest proportion of the Australian population regarded as living below the poverty line. Given that only about 40 per cent of divorced fathers contribute to the maintenance of their wives or their children in this country, most single mums have no option other than to take on the role that their husband played in their marriage. Some of the advantages of being single are denied these women or made difficult to attain because the needs of their children tend to encroach on their freedom to choose.

## The older woman

If you are a woman who was brought up in an era when appropriate behaviour for the different sexes was clearly defined and maintained – and especially if you have never worked – don't be surprised if you find the going tough. Even if in a financially comfortable position, the problems older women experience adjusting to being single can be particularly difficult. Recognising and calling upon your more masculine resources is challenging. Discovering that you can manage on your own, can be the source of tremendous satisfaction.

## Some singular lessons

If you are a single woman you are in a far better position than most who are married to explore and use your individual talents without feeling guilty. If you have close female friends many of your needs for companionship and intimacy may be met through them. Because of your upbringing, you are undoubtedly able to look after yourself in terms of domestic duties. As long as you can support yourself financially you are well able to keep house without a spouse!

Even if you would like to develop a partnership, remember that if you develop your individuality and marshal your resources now, while a free spirit, you will be less likely to saddle any man who comes into your life with your own repressed male attributes. You will, instead, be able to recognise and appreciate them in yourself and value and love the man for who he is rather than for who or what you expect him to be.

# CO-CAPTAINS ... A NEW BREED OF RELATIONSHIP

Ann is an example of a new breed of woman who has come to terms with much of her masculine energy without losing the attributes that make her feminine. From her wholeness flows much of the pleasure that she gives and receives in her relationships.

As she lives now, Ann belongs to a new breed of women. She is independent, successful in the material sense, and leads a happy and fulfilled life. She does not depend upon a man to determine the way she lives her life or for her sense of self-worth. This, however, was not always the case.

At 37, as she reflects on her life to date she believes she has benefited from the options that have become more readily available as a result of the women's liberation movement. But she is not a militant feminist. This may be because from childhood she was encouraged to assume she would have a successful career and be able to do whatever she wanted. Currently she has a growing personnel consultancy and she enjoys the material security and the advantages that a comfortable income make possible.

She has always been popular with men and as she grew up she had always seen the men in her life, be they colleagues or lovers, as friends and equals. In her mid-twenties, she met Ray, a medical student, and fell head-over-heels in love.

They began living together and things started to change. Falling in love for Ann proved to be at the expense of loving her self.

Sharing her life with Ray created difficulties. They were very different. He demanded that she fit in with his likes and dislikes and she found this hard to come to terms with. However, during the first year or two of their intense emotional involvement, she did not pay much heed to how drastically her way of life had altered. Without realising it, she lost contact with people she cared for and stopped doing things that gave her pleasure.

Four years into their relationship she could no longer avoid admitting to herself that things were very wrong. The intensity of the relationship had gone, but Ann still greatly cared for Ray. Yet she had to face the fact that by subjugating her needs for his, her enjoyment of life had waned; she had even lost much of the confidence she had had in her career. Instead of growing in the relationship she felt she had diminished as a person.

When I first met Ann she had gone through the difficult process of breaking her bond with Ray. But she was unsure how to start living again. Now many months later after having taken stock of herself, Ann is one of the most well-balanced women I have met and her lifestyle reflects this. Unlike many successful career people, she knows how to cut off at the end of a working day. Her needs to achieve are given full expression while she is at the office. Although she is quite prepared to work somewhat unusual hours she ensures that her private life receives the attention she believes it deserves.

What is more, she consciously nurtures the relationships that are important to her. She has friends who share her interests. She also makes sure that she has one or two nights at home alone to catch up with herself.

There is now another man in her life. Yet even though she cares deeply for Geoff, she doubts whether she will commit herself again to a 'living together' or exclusive partnership. Neither of them is interested in conforming to the traditional model of a marriage, nor do they want to own each other.

## A new breed of man

In Geoff, Ann has met a man who has sufficient confidence as a person in his own right not to be threatened by the fact that she cares a great deal for other people as well as for him. Unlike Ray, he appreciates that through her career she can develop her masculine side. Because of his own inner strength and security he is not jealous or possessive.

Whereas Ann has sought to express her more assertive and aggressive self, Geoff has struggled over the last years to find his feminine self. After ending two marriages in which he felt uncomfortable playing the role of husband and provider for a dependent partner, he decided to seek counselling.

After many months of introspection and distress he came to terms with his own ability to feel and share, and acknowledged his weaknesses as well as his strengths. He recognised that he had been stifling important parts of himself as he tried to be what both he and his partners had thought a good husband should be.

He regards his sharing with Ann as one of interdependence. Though they both see themselves as successfully single, these two are bonded in an intimate friendship that may well provide more happiness and outlast the usual contractual or exclusive partnerships of their friends.

# THE NEW MYTHMAKERS
## ... A WARNING

While there are no traditional guidelines to follow as a single person, there are innumerable images conveyed through the media as to what unattached people should aspire. I believe that if you want to create a happy and meaningful single life it is important to be aware of the pressures that may influence you in ways that might not be in accord with your personality, needs and aspirations.

Nowadays singles are being told they are the beautiful people. Instead of being depicted as unfortunate, unattractive or unwanted, the single is encouraged to seek a lifestyle that is affluent, hedonistic, permissive and glamorous. The brains behind advertising and marketing campaigns have transformed the picture of what it is to be without a partner. Increasingly, the vulnerabilities of the person alone add up to big business.

Open the pages of a magazine directed at the upwardly aspiring single fellow who wants to be successful with women and you witness the pressure placed on him to drive a Porsche, wear Gucci shoes, sip Veuve Cliquot and own a Vogue-style apartment.

Purveyors of perfume, make-up, lacy underwear and haute couture clothing use sexy advertising to prey upon the deep desires that single women are supposed to have. Holiday resorts offer a feast of sun, sand, sea and sex to singles on the premise that free spirits would not hestitate to exchange a fistful of dollars for the fun and instant intimacy promised.

Not only is the single ready prey to the promises of happiness promoted through the media, such advertising can also cause those who are in relationships to feel dissatisfied, to imagine that life would be much more exciting and pleasurable if they were fancy free – the grass is greener syndrome.

Now that the leisure and luxury industries are awake to the spending ability of those who do not have the responsibilities of family living, it is not surprising that they are busily creating myths in order to attract the single person's dollar. Of course the more that single people feel a need to conform to these pressures, the more successful the new mythmakers will be.

## Let's question assumptions

How do you avoid being led up blind alleys by those who have a vested interest in telling you who you are and how you should live your life?

Always question the assumptions upon which messages about living singly are based. Be aware that the pressures on you to think and behave in certain ways may well be in the best interests of others and not yourself. Know that to comply can be at your expense if you do so without conscious choice.

The images often portrayed about living effectively without a partner perpetuate the assumption that happiness is achieved when our material and sexual appetites have been whetted and satisfied, if only temporarily. However, the reality is that human needs cannot be truly satisfied by the purchasing power of the dollar or through sexual contact. Our natural cravings for warmth, care, love, acceptance, intimate communication and emotional security are of themselves intangible.

So how do we find our paths, how do we sort out the

'shoulds' from our real needs? One of the most effective ways is to confront ourselves. By answering honestly the questions set out in the following section we can begin the process that allows us to take greater control of our lives and understand ourselves.

# 2

A singular workbook

# YOUR EXPECTATIONS

*T*he following exercises encourage you to take stock of your life up to the present. As you consider your attitudes to yourself, to your life and towards being single, and the people and experiences in your past that have influenced your present circumstances, it is likely that you will become aware of areas in your life that you want to change or develop to gain more happiness and satisfaction. Such a solid basis of information about yourself will assist you to develop strategies to achieve what you want.

If you are to live effectively and happily, single or otherwise, it is invaluable for you to take such a look at yourself, your life and your relationships. Some of the questions have already been raised in previous chapters. However, now I suggest you commit your answers to paper as you read. I recommend you use an exercise book or looseleaf folder (which will be referred to as your workbook) to which you can return at any stage in your life. By so doing you can observe the changes in your attitudes and experiences that take place as you steer your course through the days, months and years ahead.

As you respond to the questions and think about the answers that other single people have given, remember that there are no rights or wrongs. It is your perceptions that are important. We can learn so much about ourselves if we are prepared to look through the eyes of others who, though different to us, experience similar challenges.

Take your time and enjoy the journey before you.

## WHY AM I READING THIS BOOK?

The reasons why you want to explore living successfully as a single are likely to be influenced by your age, your background, your past relationships and life experiences, your attitudes to yourself and your approach to life and the goals you hold for your future. You may find that the motives you have for reading this book and thinking about your life are similar to some of those given by participants in one of my Being Single seminars.

Julie, an attractive young woman, told the group without hesitation why she had come. She had recently started work with an advertising agency after completing a graphics course at college. Now that she was able to support herself financially, Julie was planning to move out of her family home. Though she looked forward to marrying one day, she was determined to live happily and effectively as a person on her own. Before she settled down she wanted to be confident in her career and to have lived and worked overseas. Julie said that she wanted to learn the 'how to's' of living as a single.

Megan sat beside her. She is a sophisticated-looking woman in her mid-thirties and from what she had told us during preliminary introductions she could have provided a good model of how to live successfully as a single for Julie. We knew that she held a responsible and demanding position in the Public Service and that she liked her work and the lifestyle it made possible for her to have. She said that she'd always been single although she had had a number of important relationships with men and liked male company.

Despite being generally happy with herself and the way she lived her life, she nevertheless wondered at times if she were really 'doing it right'. Most of her friends had married and she was the only one of her family who had remained single. She thought she had come to the seminar to hear how other people experienced life without being one of a couple. As Megan spoke about not having clear guidelines as to the way a single person should live, several heads nodded in agreement.

Tony, a small, bearded man who looked to be in his fifties was quick to respond to Megan's remarks. He, too, felt unsure as to how to live singly. Like Julie he was at the beginning of a new phase in his life yet, unlike the excitement this young woman had said she felt about her future, Tony openly acknowledged feeling anxious and pessimistic about what lay ahead. As he told us that his marriage of 33 years had come to an abrupt end with the unexpected death of his wife 18 months before, it was obvious that he was having considerable difficulty adjusting to being on his own.

Dan, who was sitting across the table from Tony, knew how it was to feel totally at a loss at the prospect of living singly. He told us that though he was only in his early thirties, he had also experienced the ending of a long-term relationship.

Dan had left his family home at the age of 20 to marry his college sweetheart. When she had suddenly deserted him for another man he had been unprepared for living on his own or fending for himself. He would later tell us that he had no desire to stay single but that at the same time he feared being vulnerable and hurt that way again.

A petite white-haired woman agreed with Dan's comments about not wanting to live as a single. Moira had previously told us that she was a divorcee with grown-up children and that she worked as a nursing sister. She was resigned to the fact that her chances of finding a mate seemed remote. As she saw it, Dan had youth on his side whereas the statistics were stacked against her, given that she would turn 58 the following year and available men were scarce.

She said that she had come to the seminar because she did not want to retire into unhappy nothingness. Like Julie she was determined that she would live as successfully as she could, be this with or without a mate. She too was looking for guidelines.

Then Di addressed the group. She said that as far as

meeting a mate was concerned, she rated the chances for an attractive, independent woman of 58 higher than those of a rather large 42-year-old mother of three.

Spending most hours of a day working to support her family or being mother, father, friend or housekeeper to her delightful but demanding brood, she had little time or opportunity left for socialising. Di told us that she hadn't been out with a man since her husband left her some four years before. Her social life was restricted to an occasional dinner or a night at the theatre with her female friends.

Despite the limitations of being a single parent, she found her children a great source of satisfaction and happiness. But she wanted to have a life of her own now, rather than put her own needs as a person aside until the children were adults.

As Di saw it, coming to the seminar was a gift to herself, a few hours set aside for the luxury of thinking about how she might make more of her life and relationships as a single woman, as well as a parent.

A tall, distinguished man in his late forties whose tailored suit and tie contrasted with the casual clothes the rest of us wore, cleared his throat and started to speak. It was not surprising to learn that he was a business executive with a multinational corporation. He seemed rather uncomfortable about being at the seminar and said that he was there out of curiosity. He didn't really regard himself as single because despite being separated from his wife for several years he was still legally married.

As we were to discover during that day, Stephen believed that he'd had his chance to make a marriage work and that he had failed. He knew how to be successful in the business world and he was willing to be a workaholic. Yet when he spoke about 'being married to his work' as the source of satisfaction in his life there was a sadness in his voice. Underneath his words could be heard emotions that he feared to face, feelings that he dare not expose, even to himself.

Stephen's comments struck a responsive chord in Kate who had been sitting quietly. Her willowy figure, finely chiselled features and richly resonant voice are familiar to theatre audiences.

Kate told us that although it might seem surprising, she

saw in Stephen's statements a reflection of her own dilemma. She had come to the seminar because she felt at a crisis point about what she wanted out of her life and her career.

From childhood she had assumed that one day she would meet a mate and have a family of her own. Now at 39 she realised that she had never really had a serious relationship. Her commitment to her work had been so demanding of her time, energy and emotions that the years had passed by without her worrying much about the void in her personal life. Yet as she approached the peak of her career with invitations to act with companies abroad, she was aware that her time for childbearing was coming to a close.

For Kate the question seemed to be whether being married to her work meant staying single and childless, and being 'left on the shelf'.

Phil had not yet given his reasons for being present and I wondered whether he was feeling pressured. I knew that he had only recently mastered a speech defect he'd had since a boy and I hoped his stammer would not hinder his desire to share with us.

After reading to himself the responses he had written in his workbook to my initial questions, Phil looked up and in an even, measured manner, spoke with barely a falter. He seemed at ease with the group.

He told us that he had come to the seminar as a step towards changing his way of life from that of a loner to one where his need for companionship and for intimate friendship could be met. He said that he felt socially backward because his speech impediment had prevented him from mixing easily. Although his chosen occupation as a computer programmer had not been dramatically hampered by the difficulties he'd had communicating, in terms of relationships Phil regarded himself more like a young teenager than a 30-year-old. He now wanted to make up for what he saw as lost time.

After he had finished speaking I asked everyone present to think about their expectations of the day ahead of us. They then wrote these goals in their workbooks before sharing them with the rest of the group.

In the same way I suggest that you now jot down in

your workbook what you would like to gain from reading *Successfully Single*. It may well be that when you reach the final pages of this book you find you have discovered something different to what you had initially expected.

## WHAT DO I WANT TO GAIN FROM THIS EXPLORATION OF MYSELF AND BEING SINGLE?

As each person in the group gave their summary it was apparent that there were as many similarities as there were differences in their individual expectations. Reading their responses could help you to clarify your own. . .

Moira briefly and clearly stated that she wanted to leave at the end of the day well on her way to developing a plan for living fully and happily in her retirement – with or without a man.

Stephen spoke next. He said he hadn't written anything, that he'd had trouble coming up with a specific goal. He nevertheless added that there was no doubt that he would like to get more enjoyment out of life outside his work. I suggested that he write this observation as a preliminary statement, as something he could revise or add to during the seminar. Again I would recommend that, as you read, you record any thoughts that come to mind so that you don't lose them. They are valuable points to which you can later return.

Kate said that she also wasn't exactly sure of what she wanted out of the day. Yet as she spoke it was apparent that she wanted to discover whether she could combine her career with being a wife and mother. She acknowledged that she felt alarmed that she may in fact remain single. This anxiety was something she would like to explore.

Tony's initial expectation of the seminar was to gain some insights into how he might now build a life for himself without his wife and live happily on his own. He could not imagine another woman in his life, yet he was lonely.

Di wasn't sure that she wanted to marry again. Yet, she said she did not want to spend the next years of her life without a man. In her case it wasn't a question of remaining single to further a career, as in Kate's instance. Her job as a telephonist was merely a means of making enough money to support her family. Her concern was how she could meet a compatible male and develop a relationship while also raising her children. With a laugh she surprised some of the group by adding that she didn't much enjoy sex on her own.

Julie hoped that the seminar would boost her confidence about moving out of home. She wanted to develop strategies for a rewarding, independent life path and to achieve her goals for work and travel. In the longer term she wanted to marry and raise a family and she did not doubt that she would do so.

Dan prefaced his aims by stating that, like Julie, he expected to have a partner. Similarly he wanted to use the day to devise ways of getting more satisfaction while living alone. He added that, even more importantly, he wanted to use this single phase in his life to regain his confidence.

Dan wanted to overcome the doubts that were the legacy of his marriage. When he met the right woman he was determined to have a happier and more enduring relationship. With some embarrassment, he added that his unhappiness when his marriage ended was compounded by the fact that he came from a Jewish family – for him, divorce had been synonymous with shame, a fceling he wanted to leave behind.

We listened to Megan next. She reiterated her need for reassurance about the way she was living her life. While it may have seemed strange to the others present, I was not surprised to hear her say that at times she felt guilty because she was content with her life. Such feelings worry many people who are otherwise happy to be single. Megan wanted to clarify whether or not she was selfish, or abnormal enjoying her single lifestyle and not wanting to have a husband and family. She said that, like Dan, she wanted to rid herself of doubts about her lifestyle that were associated with religion. Although non-practising, she still saw herself as a Catholic. Her upbringing had prepared her for being a good wife and mother or for remaining virginal rather than for delighting in sexual friendships without commitment.

Again, Phil spoke last. He told us that he hoped to learn how to relate more closely with people and develop satisfying friendships now that he no longer stammered. He was especially keen to learn how to become more comfortable with women.

HOW DO YOUR REASONS FOR READING SUCCESSFULLY SINGLE AND YOUR EXPECTATIONS COMPARE WITH THOSE GIVEN BY THE MEN AND WOMEN IN THE SEMINAR?

## Are you single again?

After a relationship comes to an end one or both partners is often cut-off, not only from the sharing they once had together but also from the network of friends and activities they had while a couple. In our group, Di, Dan, Tony and Stephen had all experienced the isolating consequences of becoming single.

## Have you been widowed?

Maybe like Tony you are grieving for someone you loved, for a relationship that brought you much happiness and which gave a sense of purpose and meaning to your life. If you have been widowed don't be surprised if you are finding it hard to live on your own, to change the familiar patterns of the life you shared while coupled. No one can replace the person you have lost, but the space that is now empty in your life can, indeed, be filled again.

What a couple have together is the combination of two unique individuals; this cannot be replicated. However, as you adjust to being on your own, a new world of possibilities for sharing opens up. Bear this in mind as you consider these exercises.

## Are you separated?

If so, you may see some similarities between Stephen's position and your own. Even if it is quite some time since your separation, you too may be denying that you are in fact single. Don't be surprised if, like Stephen, you haven't expressed your emotions and have, instead, invested your energy in doing things like working an 80 hour week to help escape your pain. It may well be that you have remained relatively unstressed on the outside since the break-up because you have really denied it has come to an end. Blocking your emotions and denying that the relationship no longer exists can cripple your life.

It is natural to grieve when a relationship ends. For some of us this is extremely difficult. Stephen decided during the seminar that he would seek one-to-one counselling to help him come to terms with the feelings he had buried deep within himself. Such assistance could be of value to you too if you want to move on from your past.

## Are you single and a parent?

Adjusting to the challenges of establishing new friendships and a single way of life can be compounded by the responsibilities of being a parent. Di's predicament of being socially isolated because of her commitments to maintaining a home and family is common. Perhaps similar circumstances have prompted you to read this book. If so, I would like you to just focus on yourself. Think about yourself as a person in your own right, about your own needs, aspirations and expectations. Later we can look to the practicalities of serving as both mum and dad to your offspring.

## Have you always been single?

If you are accustomed to living singly like Phil, Julie, Megan or Kate you are not adjusting to life without a partner. Perhaps you are now realising that some of the assumptions you have held about your future may not, in fact, eventuate.

Like Kate you may have thought that one day you would inevitably meet the Knight on the White Charger or the Enchanting Fair Maiden. But now you may be questioning your assumptions about meeting a soulmate and having children. Recognising this may require your making some significant changes in your perceptions of yourself and your way of life.

Remember Moira's determination to make the most of her future regardless of whether she met a mate? She serves as a sound model. It does not make any sense to let your desire for a partner or offspring detract from your appreciation of what you have in your life.

Maybe, like Megan, you find being single well suited to your temperament, personality and life goals. Yet being content with life without a partner goes against the mainstream of thinking and convention in our society and can cause other people to feel uncomfortable.

If you are reading these pages in quest of guidelines because of pressures you feel against your being single, realise that these guidelines are yours to write. The formula for your own happiness lies within you. Know that you do not need to feel anxious or guilty because you live as a single – no matter how disquieting it is for anyone else.

For Julie and Phil, the challenge of being single was clearly associated with that of asserting themselves as individuals. Both were on the brink of establishing independent lives for the first time away from the family home. Regardless of your age and life experience, however, developing your individuality is a challenge and it is surely a continuing life process.

An interesting question to ask yourself is:

## AM I SINGLE THROUGH CHOICE OR CIRCUMSTANCE?

Often the automatic response to this question is 'circumstance'. Only Julie and Megan in our seminar said that they were without a partner through choice.

It is easy to feel that we are on our own through circumstance if a marriage or a relationship has come to an end against our wishes, as it had for Tony, Dan, Moira, Stephen and Di, or if we haven't met the person of our dreams as Phil and Kate could say. It is also common for this response to be given because most of us have been led to believe that we should be partnered, that somehow there is something wrong with being single.

However, when you think about your answer, maybe like many of the seminar participants, you will realise that you have chosen to be single rather than commit yourself to an unsatisfactory relationship or be coupled because your parents or friends think that you should be.

When Di thought about this question she immediately responded that she was, indeed, single through the circumstance of her divorce. But, she realised on reflection that she had not taken any active steps to meet men since her husband had left her. In some ways she had chosen to remain single. As we would learn later, Di had doubts about her attractiveness and it was safer to be a housebound single mum than risk rejection. She knew that there were organisations she could go to where she could socialise with men in a similar predicament but she had not been prepared to take this step.

## Are you partnered?

It could be that you are reading *Successfully Single* because you are in a relationship but thinking about leaving it. If you are attached and fantasising about the freedoms of being single, the next question is particularly relevant. As you will discover from the responses of some of the seminar participants, there are many advantages to being single – but these are enjoyed at a price. It is up to you to determine what you are prepared to pay for the freedoms and independence a single lifestyle can provide. As you write your answers to the next question, don't censor yourself, rather create as many positive opportunities for yourself as you can.

WHAT ARE THE ADVANTAGES YOU CAN SEE IN BEING SINGLE ?

Some people find it easy to list a whole ream of advantages in being single. In the seminar, Julie, the young woman who was embarking on an independent way of life, wrote for several minutes. The advantages she eagerly shared with the group included: the freedom to come and go as she pleased, to have visitors whenever she liked, to eat whatever and whenever she wanted, to be able to decorate to her own taste, to play music and watch television programs that did not conflict with the preferences of her parents. She wanted to express herself, her individuality. Given that she had lived with her family it is no wonder that she thought being single would mean being unfettered by the restraints of family life.

As Kate spoke she told us that she had taken these advantages of being her own person for granted. Hearing Julie reminded her that she too had once eagerly anticipated the freedom to be herself. Yet she added that she now realised that she had not really been free, that her commitment to the demands of her career since adolescence had probably been as restrictive as any relationship. There was no doubt that an advantage of being single was the liberty she'd had to dedicate most of her life to acting. There had been nothing to stop her from working the long and irregular hours demanded or to do the extensive travelling required. Her work had been taxing but she had never had to worry how the pressures of her job would affect anyone else. Kate was now asking herself: 'Independence at what price?'.

## ARE THE ADVANTAGES OF LIVING SINGLY TO DO WITH FEELING INDEPENDENT?

Independence can signify different things to different people. Depending upon your own personality, your attitudes and life experience, to be independent may mean the freedom to have close friends of both sexes, to be able to be alone when you so choose, to have different sex partners, to be free of the financial responsibilities that a relationship can bring or to do simple things like reading and munching an apple in bed in the middle of the night without disturbing anyone else.

## WHAT DOES BEING INDEPENDENT MEAN TO YOU?

Everyone will answer this question differently. At the seminar, Tony interrupted Kate as she explained what independence meant to her. That she valued not having to worry about how her actions might affect another person didn't make sense to him. It was this very lack of having someone else to consider that made him feel his life was without meaning or significance. Tony's point is one that is often expressed by men and women who are not used to living without a partner. He had every right to feel this way.

Yet Tony was in a difficult position at the time of the seminar. While he couldn't imagine another woman coming into his life, he also could not see purpose or significance unless there was someone special to consider. Tony felt conflict because his need to share made him feel disloyal.

There is no doubt that in living singly you are free to

be in charge of much of the direction that your life and your relationships take. This freedom, as Tony was finding, can be difficult to adjust to if you are used to having a partner. As he listened to the experiences of others during the day, Tony realised that being single did not necessarily mean being alone. He started to see the possibilities his life now held for developing new friendships and interests. He began to think he could make changes in his lifestyle that would help to satisfy his need to share, without feeling disloyal to his deceased spouse.

Maybe like Tony you are finding it difficult to think of any advantages because you have been very happy in a relationship. However, if you are prepared to expand the way you think, the possibilities for satisfaction will emerge.

The next question is one which could take a lifetime answering. . .

## WHO AM I ?

To create the life you want, it is vital that you have a strong sense of identity. As already stated, unless you have this understanding of yourself and your needs and expectations you are unlikely to have really satisfying relationships or a life that realises your potential for happiness.

We are all unique individuals. We differ in the way we think, feel and behave at any time, according to our moods, intentions, environment and life circumstances.

I believe we are all, like diamonds, many-faceted. Yet we each have a core that makes us essentially our unique self. As you think about yourself you may find that some parts of you seem to have been obscured from view or have become dulled or out of focus. You may see aspects of yourself that need 'a polish' if they are to shine and add sparkle to your life and those who share it with you.

As you ask yourself these questions you may well discover that your core has sometimes been concealed and that the faces you show to the world do not reflect how you are inside. If there is a great deal of contradiction between your core and the way you express yourself it is likely that you will find it difficult to feel really close to anyone. The sense of isolation that can result when what we do and say do not express what we really want to convey can make us lonely. This loneliness may result regardless of whether we are single or in a partnership.

As you think about who you are, imagine how someone close to you might describe you. This person could be a parent, a friend or a lover. They may be someone you knew in the past or a person who is in your life now. Sometimes it is easier to look at yourself through someone else's eyes than through your own. Much of the impression you have of yourself is likely to have been influenced by the reactions that others have had to you.

WHO HAS BEEN CLOSE TO YOU?
HOW WOULD THEY DESCRIBE YOU?

These questions may tell you something about how much of your core you have been prepared to reveal and which facets you have shown the people around you. This information can help you to understand how you communicate and perhaps how you might express yourself more effectively.

When Kate considered this exercise she looked at herself through the eyes of the person with whom she had had most continual contact, her theatre company's director. She regarded him as a good friend as well as a source of professional guidance and support.

When Kate described herself from his viewpoint, she was ambitious, persevering, outgoing, dedicated, flexible, a perfectionist, successful, independent, confident and self-disciplined. She did not disagree with these observations, but thought that she had hidden from him – and from herself – facets that she now needed to satisfy. She realised that perhaps she had learned to act too well for her own good.

To meet the expectations of her job Kate had developed an ability to stand on her own and cope with tremendous pressure. For perhaps the first time she now acknowledged she wanted to be interdependent in a relationship. She wanted to love and to be loved and to look after and be looked after as well as being the strong talented actress who was centre stage in her career.

Stephen had difficulty with this question and said that when he tried to think of someone close to him his mind went blank. Even though he had been married for many years he didn't regard his wife as having been close. Thinking about this later in the day, he said that he suspected that many of the problems in their relationship had resulted from his inability to let his wife see or touch his core.

Stephen now feared that he would never be able to let anyone see who he was on the inside. He had built such a protective wall around himself that he was not sure that he really knew himself. Fortunately by recognising the barrier between his core and the way he presented himself he had reached a turning point. He was now in a position to breakthrough and bring an end to an emptiness he had felt inside for as long as he could recall.

Stephen is an example of someone who has lacked real closeness even though in a long-term partnership.

HAVE YOU EVER FELT REALLY CLOSE TO ANYONE ?

DO YOU HAVE ANYONE IN YOUR LIFE NOW WHO IS A FRIEND AND CONFIDANT ?

If you have always been single, chances are that it may also be hard for you to think of someone who really knows you. It is not uncommon for people who live singly to say that they have not felt particularly close to anyone since childhood and therefore have not had the opportunity to reveal more than a couple of facets of themselves. They would be described differently according to their particular role at any time – they show different aspects according to whether they are at work, at their tennis club or with their drinking mates.

Many people feel lonely because they are unable to share what they really think and feel, to communicate their doubts and dreams to someone who cares. As a single person it is imperative to have at least one friend who is a confidant, someone with whom you can be yourself. It is through such a relationship that you can come to see and appreciate your unique characteristics and potentialities. Through trust you can expose important parts of your self that may otherwise waste away in a shadow.

I cannot overemphasise the importance of taking conscious steps to develop such close friendships. I also want to remind you of the valuable, platonic, sharing you can have with people of your own sex. It is likely that they have also experienced some of the challenges you find in your life and can understand how you feel.

WHEN YOU THINK ABOUT HOW YOU DESCRIBED YOURSELF THROUGH SOMEONE ELSE'S EYES, WOULD YOU AGREE WITH THIS PICTURE ?

Perhaps like Kate you feel that important parts of you haven't been seen by this person because you haven't revealed them. This might be because of the nature of your relationship or it could be that you have concealed yourself as a way of protecting your vulnerabilities – as Stephen had done for so long. If you disagree with the description it is valuable to ask yourself why? Your answer might tell you things you haven't realised about how you communicate and about what you might like to change or develop so that you can feel more yourself in your close relationships.

As you consider yourself through another's eyes, be aware of that person's point of view. While we can learn a great deal about ourselves from the reactions that others have to us we must never forget that their values, attitudes, needs and expectations are not likely to be identical to our own.

How someone else sees us can be quite off the mark, reflecting their desire to influence, manipulate or hurt us, be this conscious or otherwise. Their perceptions can be damaging and restrict our potential for happiness.

When Di described herself she did so through the eyes of her ex-husband. Most of the adjectives in her list were to do with her appearance – and they were negative. Obviously Di's large frame and figure had borne the brunt of criticism during her marriage. As the seminar progressed Di later acknowledged to the group that she doubted that any man would want a relationship with her because she was 'fat' and 'matronly' and 'a sexual turnoff'.

Regardless of the way in which her husband had seen her, for Di the outcome of their relationship was a sadly unattractive self-image – and one that Dan was quick to point out, wasn't true. Nowhere in the description she gave us was there any reference to the warmth, humour and caring that she would display to us during that day.

If you have experienced the traumas of separation or divorce don't be surprised if like Di you feel negative about yourself. It is all too easy to have our perceptions of ourselves distorted because of difficulties in a relationship. It is common for one or both partners at the end of a marriage to see themselves as unattractive, undesirable and inadequate because of the negative descriptions they gave and received during unhappy times together.

There may well be some truth to the criticisms levelled at us during unhappy times. Undoubtedly each of us has facets that may be less than beautiful. Unfortunately these less attractive aspects can cloud our positive qualities. If we allow them, those who are important to us can make us focus on our imperfections instead of helping us to reflect our beauty.

Now list ten things you like about yourself. Don't be surprised if you find it strange or difficult to focus on your strengths rather than on your weaker points.

WHAT ARE TEN THINGS I LIKE ABOUT MYSELF ?

This list is something you can return to and add to whenever more of your attributes come to mind. In the seminar only Kate and Megan were able to write ten positive self-descriptions. Di laughed as she said that it would have been far easier for her to list her shortcomings. I suspect that Di's words reflect how most of us feel. Unfortunately we have been encouraged to see the minuses rather than the pluses in ourselves and our lives.

It is interesting to note whether the things that you value in yourself are more to do with your appearance, personality, attitudes or achievements – or something else. A little later when you complete your lifeline you may realise some things about why these aspects of yourself are positive in your eyes and why you find it difficult to recognise other aspects of yourself that are just as valuable.

Without emphasising negatives, now respond to the following questions:

ARE THERE THINGS ABOUT YOURSELF YOU'D LIKE TO CHANGE ?

IF SO, WHAT ?

WHY ?

WHAT'S STOPPING YOU ?

There's nothing wrong with wanting to make changes in ourselves and our lives. Indeed it is vital for us to realise that we have the power to alter patterns of thought and behaviour that are negative and impede our happiness. However, it can be damaging if we try to be what others want us to be at the expense of our core self.

When you think about the reasons you have for changing, be aware of what underlies your motives. Do you want to be different because someone else says you should be or because you do not feel happy within yourself?

When Di answered these questions she said that the thing she wanted to change about herself was her size. Her motive was her desire to be attractive to men. As we have seen, her husband had told her that being large meant being plain and sexually undesirable. Yet as Di thought about this she could see that her attractiveness could not be dependent solely upon her size. In fact she was no larger during her marriage than she had been when she had met her husband or when they had parted. The extra few kilograms that she was carrying now she had put on after their separation.

When the men in the group told Di that they found her attractive she admitted that she was probably protecting herself by her extra weight. Being heavier made her even more unattractive in her own eyes and protected her from the possibility of another painful relationship.

Undoubtedly Di could have shed a few kilos and one of her aims at the end of the seminar was to do exactly that. However as long as her self-assessment was governed by her husband's hurting words, it was unlikely that Di would really value herself.

The changes that Phil wanted to make also related to self-esteem. He wanted to be able to socialise more comfortably. He recognised similarities between Di's weight and his stammer: he had hidden behind his speech defect and this had sheltered him from the very thing he wanted most – to feel close to people. Di's anxiety about her figure served to shield her from her heart's desire – a lover. Now Phil no longer stammered he too had to face up to his fear that no one would really want to be close to him or find him attractive.

DO YOU HIDE BEHIND SOMETHING THAT HINDERS YOUR GETTING CLOSE TO ANYONE?

DO YOU HAVE BARRIERS THAT PREVENT YOU FROM ENJOYING LIFE AS A SINGLE?

DO YOU FEEL ISOLATED FROM THE SORT OF RELATIONSHIPS YOU'D LIKE TO HAVE?

If you have said 'yes' to any or all of these questions, you may need to find ways of overcoming the obstacles that make it difficult for you to have relationships.

Those who live singly are susceptible to feelings of isolation because it is usually up to them to initiate having their needs for company met. However, the presence of another person, be they a spouse or a stranger, does not necessarily of itself give a sense of companionship and closeness. Some of the loneliest people are those who live in empty relationships.

Communication skills are vital if we are to be able to be close and intimate with each other. Unfortunately most of us are not aware of limitations in the way in which we communicate. Phil's stammer may have been a handicap but it sensitised him to the importance of developing intimate friendship. Like Phil, we too can learn a lot from most difficulties and crises in our lives. If, for example, you have experienced the distress that the ending of a past relationship can bring, you may nevertheless have become more sensitive and aware of the importance of companionship in your life. Once you have let another person know how you think and feel on a meaningful level you need never experience the terrible sense of isolation that is symptomatic of our impersonal society.

# YOUR LIFELINE

*T*his section has been designed to get you to think about yourself in the context of your own unique lifeline.

The more you can appreciate 'where you have been' in your life and relationships, the more you can determine 'where you now want to go'. For many people, taking an overview of their lives is an eye-opening, and often moving, experience.

Take a large sheet of paper for this lifeline exercise. The more space you allow, the more scope there is for writing in the memories that will come to your mind now – and in the future – about the forces that have influenced your life. Draw a line across the centre of your page. Now divide your lifeline into units of five years. Extend the line until at least 100 years. You may well be even more optimistic about the expected length of the life that is yours to live – if so I applaud you and say 'why not?'! You may need to staple some sheets of blank foolscap together. The more room you have to express yourself the better.

Using an X to represent yourself, mark on the lifeline your age. It is interesting to observe just how far along the lifeline you have journeyed to date and how much life there is still for the living.

Draw a line up from the X and then in a few words summarise the positives that come to your mind about yourself and your life as you live it now. Then draw a line down from your X and record the more negative aspects that you think of (if any). Illustrate your words if this is easier or helpful for you. This is your life you are depicting so make it as meaningful as possible.

Now think back to the first memory you can recall in your childhood and, using a line either above or below the lifeline, indicate the age when this experience occurred and whether it was positive or negative (or both). Jot down the person or people (if any) associated with this memory and why it has significance.

Continue recalling significant experiences and record them on your lifeline. Some examples might be:

starting school
reaching puberty
your first job
your first love affair
getting married
becoming divorced
going overseas
buying a home
having a child
a death in the family

While these events are common to many of us, they are nevertheless unique in how they affect our experience of ourselves. There are innumerable things that can affect the course of our lives. Record whatever it is that you consider to have been significant to *you*. Undoubtedly you will discover that it is often the seemingly small things like something said to you in childhood that can have the most lasting influence.

Through this exercise think about the forces that have shaped you, the people and things that are important to you, the events and experiences that may have furthered or handicapped your potentiality and your happiness. Once you are conscious of these influences you are then in a better position to make decisions about how much impact they are to have on your future life.

Don't be disconcerted if it takes time for your memory to start firing. It may well be that you find yourself returning to your lifeline many times as significant things surface from your subconscious. People, words and experiences long forgotten may come suddenly to mind. Welcome them, they are helpful.

Don't be alarmed either if all you can remember at first seems to be either totally positive or all negative. How you are feeling about your life right now will tend to colour your reactions and help determine the memories that readily come back from your past.

In the seminar, Tony's memories of adulthood were mostly to do with significant events in his relationship with his now deceased wife. Above the line he included their first meeting, their engagement, their marriage, moving into their first flat, buying their home, the births of their children, their overseas trips, their silver wedding anniversary. Below the line he recorded negatives such as the onset of her illness, her hospitalisation, her death – and then the grieving that had clouded his life since that day.

It is understandable that Tony's ready recall focused on his marriage, because uppermost in his mind was his loss and his sadness. Yet as he thought further, he started to draw many more lines, capturing a variety of the good things he had experienced from childhood onwards both before and after he had met his wife. As these memories came to his mind he began to see that there were satisfactions to be had that were not dependent upon his being partnered. For example, among his early memories he recalled the time he struggled to catch a large trout in the Snowy Mountains and the day he was selected to represent his school in the national debating championship. On a number of occasions during the day, Tony returned to his lifeline as more memories surfaced. This exercise would later assist him to decide what steps he would need to take to create a more satisfying life.

When Stephen spoke to the group about this exercise he told us that he hadn't thought much about his past before as he had always been more interested in the future. As he looked back over his lifeline he said that most of the significant experiences he'd recalled were what he regarded as achievements and failures along his way to success. Most of his memories were to do with school, sport and his career.

He could clearly recall when as a six-year-old his father praised him for captaining his cricket team to victory. How he'd glowed inside that day!

Sadly, that was the only memory Stephen had of either of his parents ever saying he had done anything well. Yet he could remember how later, when he won awards for sport and scholarship at college and university, his success lacked that special feeling of warmth and satisfaction he'd known that day as a boy. No matter what he achieved, he never again received the recognition from his parents that he craved.

As an adult Stephen had been rapidly promoted up the career ladder. These business successes seemed more important to him than anything else. Yet he said that they gave him little feeling of satisfaction as he was always thinking of the rung ahead.

Included among the few minuses he recorded on his lifeline were his not winning the university medal for economics on graduation and his losing a large sum of money (and his pride) when the stock market collapsed in 1980. For Stephen career goals not attained and disappointments in business constituted failures. He now acknowledged that the only emotion he was familiar with was the fear of failure. It was his anxiety about losing that motivated his strong desire to win, rather than his appreciation and enjoyment of the achievement.

People or relationships barely featured on his lifeline, and this was now obviously distressing to him. As a child his parents had told him they expected him to succeed if they were to be proud of him. They were not demonstrative people and he had no memory of their being affectionate to each other or to him. Now he realised as he looked at his past just how little anyone in his adult life had really meant to him. They had usually been a means to an end. Even his marriage had been a scoring point as his wife had been sought after by a number of eligible bachelors because of her looks and her family background. To him she had been a conquest more than the woman he loved and his mate.

He was now starting to see that though his parents had both died several years beforehand, he had been striving to gain their recognition at the expense of his feelings and those of the people in his life.

ARE YOU STRIVING TO LIVE UP TO EXPECTATIONS HELD OF YOU IN CHILDHOOD ?

Unlike Stephen, Moira's lifeline reflected memories that were more to do with her relationships than her successes. During the years of her marriage she recalled several achievements, but they were those of her children, not her own.

As she considered her lifeline and listened to what the others shared about theirs, Moira could see that she had not given any heed to her own personal achievements. Yet, like Stephen she had excelled at sport and study in her youth. She had also succeeded in her career as a nurse and was a double certificated sister before she met her husband. Yet these successes had not rated a mention.

When asked why she hadn't proudly recorded her achievements, Moira said that she thought it was because from childhood she had believed that what was important in life was for her to become a good wife and mother. Her own mother had not worked and her family had been happy and close. She attributed her own successes at school and at work more to natural ability than ambition.

Given the apparent importance of family life to her, it was interesting that Moira hadn't recorded anything positive on her lifeline about her relationship with her husband. She told us that she felt largely to blame for her failed marriage. Although it didn't now seem rational, she had felt tremendous conflict and guilt for years because she had worked to help support her family. By doing so she had believed that somehow she had undermined her husband.

Instead of being proud of her skills as a nursing sister, during her marriage Moira had come to regard her work as a source of tension. For her family to live a comfortable lifestyle she'd had no choice but to work. Her husband had not had much education and during most of their life together she had been able to earn a good deal more than him.

Despite having reared healthy and happy children she still believed that she had been inadequate as a wife and mother because she had not spent 24 hours a day at home as she 'should', as her own mother had done.

She told us how these days she obtains a great deal of satisfaction and pleasure from her work and from the recognition she receives for her ability. She seemed embarrassed about acknowledging this success.

A couple of moments later, Moira went back to her lifeline, and in a firm strong hand began to write down some of the personal successes she had not acknowledged.

HAVE YOU DENIED IMPORTANT PARTS OF YOURSELF IN ORDER TO BE WHAT OTHERS EXPECT YOU TO BE AS A GOOD SON OR DAUGHTER, WIFE OR HUSBAND, MOTHER OR FATHER, BUSINESS EXECUTIVE OR EMPLOYEE?

Don't be surprised if, like Stephen and Moira, you feel strong emotions when you look at your lifeline and think about your past. There is nothing wrong with feeling proud, sad, angry or happy as you recall incidents that were important to you. It could well be that you were unable to express your emotions at the time. Giving vent to them now can clear your system, leaving you free to move on.

DO YOU BELIEVE THAT YOU SHOULD NOT SHOW YOUR FEELINGS? WHY?

Dan was obviously embarrassed by his tears as he recalled the day his wife left him. While Megan, who was sitting beside him, put her arms around him he started to sob uncontrollably. Several minutes later he told us that these tears were the first he'd shed since he was at kindergarten. He recalled the shame he'd felt then being called a 'sissy' because he'd bawled when he fell off a bike.

As he looked at his lifeline, he could see that bottling up his feelings since that incident had helped to dull his experience of life. He had not recalled more than one or two memories in the years since his wife's departure. It was as if he had been numb to the world around him. Through his tears Dan said that he was tired of being a robot. He wanted to feel like a human being.

Unfortunately for most of us, particularly those who have an Anglo-Saxon heritage, showing our feelings – especially our strong negative emotions – can be very difficult. From early on in life we learn to hold back our tears, to 'bite our lip' instead of saying what we really think and feel. Yet it is healthy to give vent to emotions. While we need to respect the sensitivities of those around us, we nevertheless have the need and the right to be able to acknowledge what we really feel.

As babies we do not have alternative ways of letting our fear, anger and frustration be known other than through crying. As we develop we learn to communicate through words and actions what concerns us. Understandably words are a more socially acceptable and mature way of conveying what it is that we want to express. Yet in getting us to control the strong feelings that overwhelm us as youngsters, well-meaning adults can make us believe that our feelings themselves are bad and not to be revealed. It is easy for us to feel shame or guilt because we are angry, hurt, disappointed or sad, even when such emotions are logical and reasonable reactions to our circumstances.

If we develop a habit of repressing our true feelings like both Stephen and Dan it is likely that things in our past will deaden our appreciation of the present.

Looking at your lifeline can help you to appreciate the expectations and beliefs you have developed over the years about what living happily means to you. Like Stephen you may find that you have focused on achievement in a narrow sense and that this is because of what you were led to regard as important by parents, teachers or friends. Maybe you too have emphasised one aspect of your life at the expense of others because you seek recognition and approval. Yet if you are to lead a full and satisfying life a range of needs must be recognised.

How you regard being single can be influenced by beliefs held by the religious or social groups with which you identify. Megan had been reared a Catholic. Even though non-practising for years, she nevertheless felt guilty because she enjoyed sex without being married and wasn't interested in having a family.

It isn't surprising that Megan had some anxieties about being single, given that the values she had accepted as a child conflicted with what she wanted of her life as an adult. She recounted to the group one of her most negative memories – the day when at 19 her mother asked where she had failed as a parent by having a daughter who rejected her religion. Much of Megan's guilt was associated with feeling responsible for her mother's unhappiness and self-recrimination. She was perpetuating the pattern of self-blame. For Megan, staying single was yet another hurt she added to her mother's list of woes.

DO YOU FEEL GUILTY BECAUSE YOU ARE YOURSELF?
IF SO, WHY?

Maybe feeling guilty is inappropriate and you are making yourself unhappy without just reason.

# WHERE ARE YOU NOW?

*A*fter taking an overview of your life to date to assist you to gain some insights into why you hold the attitudes you have towards yourself and being single, I want you to assess where you are now in terms of your physical and emotional well-being.

Single people who live alone often have to make a very conscious effort to ensure that their physical and emotional needs are looked after. Unless they live in an institution or in a community, they cannot, as a rule, assume that anyone else is looking after their welfare, as those who are partnered often do.

Firstly, think about your physical health. Unless you are fit it is difficult to feel positive about yourself and to create a satisfying life. Those who have not been used to living singly seem to be the most likely to let themselves go as they are unused to accepting responsibility for caring for themselves.

WHAT DOES YOUR APPEARANCE SAY ABOUT HOW YOU REGARD YOURSELF?

Our outward physical appearance can tell a lot about how well each of us attends to our diet and our needs for sufficient rest and exercise. Even the attention we give to our clothing and our general presentation can be a telltale sign of how well we are accepting the responsibility of being at the helm of our lives.

## HAVE YOU LET YOUR HEALTH OR APPEARANCE SLIDE? AND WHAT ABOUT YOUR DIET?

How you feed yourself reflects how you regard yourself. Many singles will say they can't be bothered cooking unless there's someone else to cook for, forgetting that every day they need well-balanced and nutritious meals.

No matter what problems beset you, you must eat sensibly and ensure that you sleep and exercise as much as your body requires. If you are troubled by emotional problems that prevent you from eating adequately or that disturb your sleep or diminish your usual energy levels it is important that you take action. Often talking problems over with a friend, a counsellor or a doctor can help.

Your body reflects your general emotional and psychological health as well as your physical well-being. As you look over the following list of symptoms, ask yourself how often they have occurred in the past twelve months. Record your responses as they will guide you to the changes you may choose to make from today on. Don't forget that if you are not eating a nutritionally sound diet and having the sleep and exercise you need, these symptoms are far more likely to occur and to impede your enjoyment of life.

## HOW IS YOUR HEALTH?

Complete the following table, indicating whether any of the problems have affected you in the past twelve months.

| | NEVER | RARELY | OCCASIONALLY | FAIRLY OFTEN | VERY OFTEN |
|---|---|---|---|---|---|
| HEADACHES | | | | | |
| DIGESTIVE UPSETS | | | | | |
| HIGH BLOOD PRESSURE | | | | | |
| DIFFICULTY IN SLEEPING | | | | | |
| WORRY AND ANXIETY | | | | | |
| TIRING EASILY | | | | | |
| FEELING GUILTY | | | | | |
| FEELING THAT I CAN'T COPE | | | | | |
| CRYING SPELLS | | | | | |
| FEELING LONELY | | | | | |
| FEELING WORTHLESS | | | | | |
| LACK OF INTEREST OR PLEASURE IN SEX | | | | | |
| LOSING WEIGHT | | | | | |
| FEELING FAT, GAINING WEIGHT | | | | | |
| DRINKING MORE THAN USUAL | | | | | |
| SMOKING MORE THAN USUAL | | | | | |
| FEELING IRRITABLE OR ANGRY | | | | | |
| FEELING SAD OR DEPRESSED | | | | | |
| FEELING TENSE | | | | | |
| OTHER ? | | | | | |

Most of us experience some of these problems at some time in our lives. This is most likely to be the case when a crisis takes place. However, if you often have any of these symptoms or if they persist, you must take active steps to be rid of them.

WHAT STEPS HAVE YOU TAKEN TO OVERCOME THEM ?

ARE THERE ANY STEPS YOU SHOULD BE TAKING ?

It is common for doctors to prescribe drugs as a means of treating problems like depression, anxiety, sleeplessness, headaches and feeling lonely. While in many instances there is obviously a place for drug therapy it is at best a temporary aid. I believe that often people are prescribed pills by well-meaning doctors when what they really need is the healing that understanding companionship can bring. As Dr James Lynch in his book *The Broken Heart, The Medical Consequences of Loneliness* documents so clearly, loneliness or an unfulfilled desire to share is at the root of many physical symptoms of distress.

I believe friendship to be a very powerful key to resolving most of our emotional problems. Unfortunately we can be reluctant to talk about our difficulties because we fear we might 'burden' those who care about us. Yet by voicing what it is that is troubling us to a friend, and letting our emotions surface and be released, we can rid ourselves of the pressures that underlie the symptoms of our distress.

As a rule, sharing the things that worry us with a friend not only makes us feel much better but helps to bring us closer together. If you do not have anyone you feel you can turn to, there are various helping agencies that range from voluntary telephone counsellors through to professional psychologists who can help you.

Instead of being a burden to another person when you share your difficulties, you may be surprised to find that by speaking up you give them the gift of your trust . . . and they are able to give to you by listening.

Loneliness is a problem that many singles say that they experience because they do not have someone special in their lives. Yet such feelings of loneliness can result from a lack of communication skills rather than lack of a partner. In workshops I have held, it has been common for several of those present to say that they had rarely if ever felt that they had really 'connected' or been understood when they expressed things that were important to them. Such comments came from both single and partnered.

Blocks to communication can come from our believing that there is something we shouldn't say about our thoughts, our feelings, doubts, dreams and disappointments, and about our needs and expectations. If we believe it is unacceptable to talk about things that are personal, even though they are important to us, a fear of rejection can prevent us from letting anyone see how we really feel. This fear can thereby cause us to feel isolated and lonely.

The more we want to be close it seems the more we risk feeling cut off or misunderstood. It is easy to feel rejected when we have not been understood.

DO YOU EVER FEEL CUT OFF OR MISUNDERSTOOD BECAUSE YOU HAVE NOT BEEN HEARD ?

In the seminar, Phillip learned about the therapeutic power of being listened to and heard when he completed an exercise with Di. She had to listen without comment or judgment for some minutes while he told her about the things that were troubling him. All such a sharing process requires is that two people take turns to be available to each other and to listen closely.

Phillip later told us what a novel experience this deceptively simple exercise had been for him. Because he had stammered for most of his life, the significant people to him, such as his parents, had tended to speak for him. Rarely had he had the opportunity to finish sentences let alone express thoughts and emotions that were difficult to share because they were personal.

While he was talking with Di, Phillip began to stammer badly. His doubts about his attractiveness and his ability to cope independently of his parents had made him anxious. Yet Di had sat attentive throughout, without any attempt to interpret, evaluate or console; she had just listened.

We do not have to have impediments like Phillip's stammer to be interrupted mid-sentence or to have others assume that they know what we want to say. Very few people have learned the skill and the gift of listening.

## ARE YOU A GOOD LISTENER?

Kate had always thought of herself as a good communicator. Her career as an actress depended upon her ability to interpret the characters she played. So it was with surprise that she told the group that she had found it difficult not to interject and reassure Julie as they did the listening exercise together. She couldn't help wanting to make suggestions as Julie talked.

If you stop and observe people in conversation you will probably conclude that it is not easy for most of us to sit and listen without interjecting or making judgments. Automatically our minds start interpreting, reaching conclusions, coming up with answers. Such 'chatter' in our heads interferes with our hearing what is being said.

Unfortunately it is very easy for 'message sent' to be different from 'message received' because of the tendency we have to let our own thoughts and experience intrude.

## HOW CAN YOU ENSURE THAT YOU ARE REALLY LISTENING TO SOMEONE AND HEARING THEM?

When it is important that you understand how someone else feels or thinks it can be very useful to use the skill called 'active listening'. By active listening not only do you make yourself available non-judgmentally to what is being said but you also check from time to time that you are hearing correctly.

By saying something like: 'let me see if I got you right . . . what you just said was . . .' you are repeating back to the speaker what you thought you heard. They then have the opportunity to correct or clarify anything you have unintentionally interpreted or omitted. They also realise that you are giving them your attention, which is one of the most valuable gifts you can give to another person.

Our own needs can sometimes colour what we hear and confuse what is being said to us. Remember earlier in the seminar how Tony found it difficult to sit and listen as

Kate stated that not having to think about anyone else was one of the advantages of being single. Tony's own needs for love and companionship prevented him from hearing what Kate was saying about herself, and he interrupted.

If he had uncritically listened to Kate as she'd explained what independence meant to her, he would have been in a far better position to state his own ideas and feelings and establish mutual understanding. He would also perhaps have become aware of other ways of thinking that could assist him in finding more pleasure in his life as a single.

# How satisfied are you with your life now?

It is easy as a single person to live a lopsided lifestyle. There is often nothing to stop you from focusing on one or two aspects of life – be this your work, a sporting activity, a hobby or interest – to the detriment of your overall well-being. The following table will help you to recognise any changes you might like to make so that your lifestyle becomes more balanced and rewarding.

When you look over your responses, don't be surprised if there are areas in your life which need more attention. It is your becoming aware of the things that need to be developed or changed that is important.

When thinking about the levels of satisfaction you experience in various aspects of your life, and ways of adding to your enjoyment, it can be helpful to ask:

WHAT MAKES ME HAPPY ?

WHAT DO I APPRECIATE MOST IN MY LIFE?

For some people, these are not easy questions to answer. Once we know what we are after we can then devise plans to attain our goals. It is one thing to realise what we find satisfying and another to actually assume the responsibility for obtaining such pleasure.

To achieve what we want in life we need to be able to manage time effectively. So, before you devise strategies for a more rounded and rewarding lifestyle, it is valuable to make an assessment of how well you manage time. All

## AT THE PRESENT TIME I FEEL:

| REALLY PLEASED | PLEASED | SATISFIED | MIXED CONTENT | NOT CONTENT | UNHAPPY VERY | | N/A | ABOUT: |
|---|---|---|---|---|---|---|---|---|
| 1 | 2 | 3 | 4 | 5 | 6 | 7 | 8 | MY OCCUPATION |
| 1 | 2 | 3 | 4 | 5 | 6 | 7 | 8 | HOW I SPEND MY TIME |
| 1 | 2 | 3 | 4 | 5 | 6 | 7 | 8 | MY PERSONAL RELATIONSHIP |
| 1 | 2 | 3 | 4 | 5 | 6 | 7 | 8 | MY ACHIEVEMENTS |
| 1 | 2 | 3 | 4 | 5 | 6 | 7 | 8 | MY PERSONAL CIRCUMSTANCES |
| 1 | 2 | 3 | 4 | 5 | 6 | 7 | 8 | THE WAY I BALANCE MY LIFE |
| 1 | 2 | 3 | 4 | 5 | 6 | 7 | 8 | MY FRIENDS – SOCIAL LIFE |
| 1 | 2 | 3 | 4 | 5 | 6 | 7 | 8 | MY SEX LIFE |
| 1 | 2 | 3 | 4 | 5 | 6 | 7 | 8 | THE CONTRIBUTION I MAKE TO OTHERS |
| 1 | 2 | 3 | 4 | 5 | 6 | 7 | 8 | THE MEANING I FIND IN MY LIFE |
| 1 | 2 | 3 | 4 | 5 | 6 | 7 | 8 | MY HEALTH |
| 1 | 2 | 3 | 4 | 5 | 6 | 7 | 8 | THE EXERCISE AND RECREATION I TAKE |
| 1 | 2 | 3 | 4 | 5 | 6 | 7 | 8 | MY CHILDREN AND BEING A PARENT |
| 1 | 2 | 3 | 4 | 5 | 6 | 7 | 8 | WHERE I LIVE |
| 1 | 2 | 3 | 4 | 5 | 6 | 7 | 8 | MY HOME ENVIRONMENT |
| 1 | 2 | 3 | 4 | 5 | 6 | 7 | 8 | THE INTERESTS I HAVE OUTSIDE MY WORK |
| 1 | 2 | 3 | 4 | 5 | 6 | 7 | 8 | MY ABILITY TO COMMUNICATE EFFECTIVELY |
| 1 | 2 | 3 | 4 | 5 | 6 | 7 | 8 | MY PHYSICAL APPEARANCE |
| 1 | 2 | 3 | 4 | 5 | 6 | 7 | 8 | MY ABILITY TO HAVE FUN, TO ENJOY MYSELF |
| 1 | 2 | 3 | 4 | 5 | 6 | 7 | 8 | THE WAY I MANAGE TIME |
| 1 | 2 | 3 | 4 | 5 | 6 | 7 | 8 | MY APPRECIATION OF BEAUTY |
| 1 | 2 | 3 | 4 | 5 | 6 | 7 | 8 | THE QUALITY OF MY EXPERIENCE OF LIFE |
| 1 | 2 | 3 | 4 | 5 | 6 | 7 | 8 | THE EXPRESSION OF MY CREATIVITY |
| 1 | 2 | 3 | 4 | 5 | 6 | 7 | 8 | THE VALUE OF WHAT I DO FOR SOCIETY |

too often we use time as the excuse for our not being able to do the things that we'd like to. The following table has been designed to give you a picture of how you spend an average weekday and weekend. While you don't need to be precise, it is well worth trying to be as accurate as you can.

The table then asks you to repeat the same exercise (using the second set of check boxes), only this time imagine how you would like to spend a typical weekday or weekend.

When you look over your responses you may notice that you do not give much time to things you enjoy and appreciate. If the problem is really one of time, ask yourself:

HOW MIGHT I MORE EFFECTIVELY MANAGE MY TIME SO THAT I CAN ENJOY AND APPRECIATE MY LIFE MORE?

Often the obstacles are more of our own making than because there are not enough hours in a day. If we recognise these barriers for what they are, we are able to maximise our chances of doing what is really important to us. So be honest as you ask yourself:

WHAT AM I NOT DOING THAT I'D LIKE TO?

WHAT IS STOPPING ME?

ARE THESE LIMITATIONS WITHIN MYSELF OR EXTERNAL?

WHICH OF THESE DO I SEE AS SURMOUNTABLE?

HOW?

Remember how Tony realised during the lifeline exercise how much he had once enjoyed fishing? He also listed being in the countryside and appreciating the beauty of nature as something that brought him a great deal of peace and satisfaction. Yet when he answered the questions: When did I last enjoy my preferred activities? and How recently have I been consciously aware of what I appreciate most in my life?, he said that because of his wife's ill

| 1. HOW I SPEND MY TIME<br>2. HOW I'D LIKE TO SPEND MY TIME | HOURS SPENT | | |
|---|---|---|---|
| | WDAY | SAT | SUN |
| MY OCCUPATION : | | | |
| WORK-RELATED TRAVEL | ☐☐ | | |
| PREPARING, PLANNING | ☐☐ | | |
| AND WORRYING – OUT OF USUAL HOURS | ☐☐ | | |
| ACTUAL WORK | ☐☐ | | |
| RECOVERING | ☐☐ | | |
| SOCIALISING THAT IS WORK-ORIENTED | ☐☐ | | |
| WORK-RELATED STUDY | ☐☐ | | |
| OTHER............ | ☐☐ | | |
| MY RELATIONSHIPS : | | | |
| TIME WITH ACQUAINTANCES | ☐☐ | | |
| TIME WITH FAMILY | ☐☐ | | |
| TIME WITH CHILDREN | ☐☐ | | |
| TIME WITH CLOSE FRIENDS | ☐☐ | | |
| TIME WITH A SEX PARTNER | ☐☐ | | |
| TIME WITH FRIENDS WITH FAMILY | ☐☐ | | |
| OTHER........... | ☐☐ | | |
| MY RECREATION : | | | |
| RELAXING ALONE | ☐☐ | | |
| T.V. | ☐☐ | | |
| FILMS | ☐☐ | | |
| PARTIES | ☐☐ | | |
| PUBS | ☐☐ | | |
| RESTAURANTS | ☐☐ | | |
| READING | ☐☐ | | |
| SPORTS | ☐☐ | | |
| FITNESS | ☐☐ | | |
| INTERESTS | ☐☐ | | |
| OTHER............ | ☐☐ | | |
| CULTURE, EDUCATION, SPIRITUAL ACTIVITIES : | | | |
| PERFORMING ARTS | ☐☐ | | |
| CHURCH/SPIRITUAL INTERESTS | ☐☐ | | |
| POLITICAL ACTIVITIES | ☐☐ | | |
| NON-WORK ORIENTED STUDY | ☐☐ | | |
| COMMUNITY ORGANISATIONS/ACTIVITIES | ☐☐ | | |
| OTHER........... | ☐☐ | | |
| SLEEP : | ☐☐ | | |
| OTHER ACTIVITIES.......... | ☐☐ | | |

* NEED NOT ADD UP TO 24 HOURS

health years had passed since he had ventured out of the city and it had been more than three decades since he'd held a rod in his hand. Although going fishing would not resolve his sadness, Tony could see that taking the relatively simple step of getting into his car and heading into the country in quest of trout would be a way of doing something positive and pleasurable as part of a new phase in his life.

WHAT ARE SOME STEPS YOU COULD TAKE RIGHT NOW TO INCREASE YOUR LEVELS OF SATISFACTION IN LIFE?

# What values are important to you?

To determine the path you want to follow to enrich your life it is important that you are aware of the values that give quality and meaning to your experiences.

Of the following list of values choose the three that are most important to you and then the three that are least important.

---

A COMFORTABLE LIFE
A SENSE OF ACCOMPLISHMENT
EQUALITY (SOCIAL JUSTICE, EQUAL OPPORTUNITY FOR ALL)
FAMILY SECURITY (TAKING CARE OF LOVED ONES)
FREEDOM
INNER HARMONY
MATURE LOVE (PERSONAL AND SEXUAL INTIMACY)
POWER (THE ABILITY TO INFLUENCE EVENTS AND MAKE THINGS HAPPEN)
SPIRITUAL DEVELOPMENT
SELF-RESPECT
TRUE FRIENDSHIP
WISDOM
RECOGNITION (FAME)
PERSONAL GROWTH (SELF-DEVELOPMENT)
AN EXCITING LIFE
A LIFE FULL OF SENSUAL PLEASURE

The process of ranking the given values in their order of priority can tell you a lot about what is likely to give you greatest satisfaction. It can be quite revealing to then ask:

HOW DOES THE WAY I LIVE REFLECT MY VALUES ?

We can feel dissatisfied and unhappy if our lifestyle is in conflict with the values we hold. For example, if you placed a life full of sensual pleasure as most important to you and yet you currently live in a monastic environment, it is unlikely that you would be feeling especially content with your lot. Similarly, if you live as a monk yet you have indicated that spiritual development is of little importance to you, it is more than likely you are living in the wrong place.

When you compare your nominated 'most important' values with those that you have experienced, you may identify the areas on which you want to focus more attention. In the seminar Kate regarded a sense of accomplishment, mature love and true friendship as being most important to her, while power, a life full of sensual pleasure and an exciting life were the least. Yet, while the way she had lived had certainly given her much opportunity for satisfying her needs for accomplishment, she was aware that the other important values had not been met.

It is no surprise that we are dissatisfied if what we do is in conflict with what we value. For Tony the life he was leading alone seemed quite contrary to his most prized value, that of family security, of taking care of loved ones. Tony had experienced being a loving husband and father. He knew the fulfilment this had given him. As he thought about his response he acknowledged that perhaps he was being stupid to think he should live alone from now on when he so enjoyed companionship and family life. As he completed these exercises he was changing his perception of the possibilities the future held for him. He was looking happier and more relaxed.

# Influences on your life so far

For many people, especially if they're just starting to pave independent paths like Julie and Phil, parents are the ones to have influenced their life the most this far. However, even if you are in the later years of life, don't be surprised if you give a similar response, because so much of our personality and our approach to life is influenced by the initial relationships we have with those who rear us.

Perhaps for you, like for Tony, Dan and Di, the person who automatically springs to mind is an ex-partner. Or, as for Moira, it may well be that your own children figure prominently. Regardless of how long your list is and who the people are, it is valuable to ask yourself:

HOW HAVE THEY INFLUENCED HOW I SEE MYSELF?

Maybe, like Stephen, you have been striving to live up to an image of yourself that has limited your capacity to enjoy much of life. Or perhaps as in Julie's case you have confidence in your ability to create a satisfying life for yourself because of the warmth and encouragement you have received from the people who have mattered most.

Remember the negative effects that Di's husband's words about her weight had upon her self-image? Like Di you do not have to be confined by attitudes and expectations held of you by people in your past or present even if they have been, or are, immensely important to you. If you can understand how they have influenced your perception of yourself you can then choose to see yourself differently and express yourself in ways that may differ from their expectations or ideals.

For this reason it is useful also to ask:

HOW HAVE THESE PEOPLE INFLUENCED MY ATTITUDES TO BEING SINGLE?

For Megan, it was clear that the guilt she felt about enjoying her single lifestyle stemmed from the traditional Catholic convictions her family held about sex and marriage. As she thought about this, she acknowledged that for some years her parents had seemed to accept that she lived her own life. She was welcome to bring friends with her to their home when she visited and they did not ask embarrassing questions. They let her know that they loved her and were proud of her achievements. Megan could now see that her parents' love and acceptance was what counted. She realised that she didn't need to feel guilty for the way she chose to live.

Moira said that her son and daughter featured as the most important influences on her life. This was not perhaps so much of a surprise given that most of her adult years had been spent providing them with the wherewithal to become the successful and independent people of whom she was now so proud. Although they had supported her decision to leave her marriage, she doubted that they approved of her wanting to find another man.

It was her daughter who had told her that the statistics were against her meeting a suitable male at her age and who had laughingly added that a man in his sixties would not have much to offer her anyway. She had also told Moira that there was no need to worry about a mate as her recently married brother had said that he was planning to build a granny flat at the back of his home for her when she retired. By then, he thought, he'd have children and she could enjoy the pleasures of being a grandmother and babysitter.

Moira now recognised that even though she was appreciative of her son's concern, it was not what she wanted. She was prepared to live independently, alone if need be. She exclaimed that she wasn't going to resign herself to thinking that there wasn't a man who would enjoy sharing the years of later life with her. Why should she give up the pleasure that such a romantic possibility would add to her everyday existence? Like Moira you too may benefit by asking:

HAS ANYONE MADE ASSUMPTIONS ABOUT YOUR LIFE AS A SINGLE THAT YOU'D LIKE TO QUESTION?

# Learning from your past relationships

Your past offers a tremendous opportunity to assess your relationship needs. Ask yourself:

WHAT HAVE I LEARNT ABOUT WHAT RELATIONSHIPS
MEAN TO ME?

ABOUT MY VULNERABILITIES?

ABOUT MY LIMITATIONS—WHAT AM I NOT PREPARED
TO GIVE/CHANGE/COMPROMISE?

ABOUT WHAT AN IDEAL RELATIONSHIP IS TO ME?

ABOUT WHAT I AM ABLE TO GIVE IN A RELATIONSHIP
AS A SINGLE PERSON?

Dan believed he had little to give anyone at this stage
anyway. He thought that he had spent so much time bottling up his feelings that they would be overwhelming to
anyone who broke through his barriers. Yet at the same
time he could see, in retrospect, that a problem in his
marriage was that he didn't express what he felt and that
even though he loved his wife, she didn't know this. Dan
was determined now to express more of his emotions to
people to whom he wanted to be close.

Megan told Dan that the answer was simple; what he
needed was to discover the joys of friendship. She thought
he should put his desires (and his fears) about marrying
again out of his mind for a while and enjoy himself with
good company.

We already knew that Megan didn't want to marry and
that she enjoyed male company and sex. Now she told us
her ideal was to have a man or two who cared for her but
who did not want to live with her or have a full-time
relationship. She shocked some of those present when she
said that she would be quite happy if a lover was married
or had another woman in his life. What was important to
her was that he would want to spend time with her regularly but leave her free to pursue her own interests and
maintain the friendships that were important to her.

For Tony, Megan's comments about the importance of
friendship made sense, but in no way could he understand
how she could consider having a relationship with someone who was attached. He said that he didn't want to
make judgments as something he had learned that day was

that people have different needs and want different things in their lives and relationships. He thanked all of us for having helped him reach a breakthrough. His future was no longer looking so grim. He could see that what he had been missing most in his life since his wife's death was the feeling that he was close to someone. Yet there were people he knew who would appreciate his company, if only he made himself available to them – his children and grandchildren were one example. Tony's realisation pre-empted the next series of questions.

ARE YOU SATISFIED WITH THE RELATIONSHIP YOU
HAVE WITH.....

YOUR FAMILY?

YOUR FRIENDS?

YOUR COLLEAGUES AT WORK?

IF NOT, WHY NOT?

In retrospect, Kate realised that from childhood she had given very little to anyone. She felt that she had short-changed herself and those who loved her by focusing so much on her work, that it had become her life. She could see how she had taken for granted the support, encouragement and pride her parents had shown over the years just as she had somehow assumed that one day she would meet an ideal mate.

She decided that it would not take too much effort on her part to bring more warmth and happiness to her family and to herself by putting aside more time for them. She could also make herself more available to develop friendships. The opportunity for meeting interesting people through her work and travel was always there.

Most of us have people in our lives we could delight in being with if we only took the time and effort required to initiate contact and share more intimately. When you think about your own life

ARE THERE WAYS BY WHICH YOU COULD ENRICH THE
QUALITY OF THE RELATIONSHIPS YOU HAVE?

ARE THERE ANY PEOPLE YOU WOULD LIKE TO BE
CLOSER TO?

IF SO, WHAT IS STOPPING YOU FROM DEVELOPING THE
RELATIONSHIPS YOU WOULD LIKE TO HAVE WITH THEM?

It is not unusual to have a closed circle of people to
whom we feel close and as a result we tend to ignore the
chance to make new friends. Equally, many of us feel that
something is lacking in our current relationships and yet
we do nothing to change them.

DO YOU WANT TO FORM NEW FRIENDSHIPS?

IF SO, WHAT ARE YOU DOING TO MAKE THIS POSSIBLE?

For Phil these two questions were particularly relevant.
He had come into the group because he had felt isolated
and because he was willing to develop relationships. In
thinking about what he might do to start mixing and sharing with men and women who could become his friends
he welcomed various suggestions from the group like joining interest-oriented clubs or going to dancing classes. But
because of the lack of confidence he felt in his ability to
socialise, it seemed that to take such steps would be
extremely anxiety provoking . . . even though he said he
was determined to give them a go.

Julie suggested he move into a mixed household of
singles, perhaps with students or with young people who
had jobs. For him to live entirely on his own would be an
enormous step and not one that would necessarily give
him the chance to practise the skills of mixing and sharing
that he felt he so sorely lacked.

Phil was delighted with the idea of sharing accommodation. This was not surprising given that much of the
loneliness experienced by many single people is a feeling
of emptiness that living alone can bring. Even for those
who enjoy solitude, enforced aloneness can be difficult to
handle.

ARE THERE WAYS BY WHICH YOU COULD CHANGE YOUR
LIVING ARRANGEMENTS TO OBTAIN MORE
SATISFACTION OF YOUR NEEDS?

# YOUR EPITAPH

*A*t the end of the seminar I suggest that each person think ahead to the end of their life and imagine how they would ideally like to look back on their years. This exercise can help to put what you want your life to be in perspective.

19__ to ____

———— will be remembered as a person who

_____

_____

_____

# A Review

Only one exercise now remains to complete. Turn back to your initial statement of expectations. Consider whether they have changed in some way through the course of the exercises. It could be that like Di the emphasis for you has shifted from wanting to meet a mate to learning to know and value yourself more. Or perhaps, as for Tony, you no longer think you are doomed to live a life of loneliness and now want to bring joy to your life and to the people you share it with.

Dan's aims were still the same in that he wanted to overcome the doubts and feelings of shame he'd harboured since his marriage ended. Yet he could see that for the present his prime objective was to 'start bringing his inside out', to let people see how he really felt, to learn how to be close.

Stephen had realised during the day that there was nothing to be ashamed of in being single and that he would take divorce action so that his wife could be free to start a new single life for herself.

At the outset Stephen had half-heartedly written that his aims for the day were to get more enjoyment out of life and work. But before he could do so, he had to unlearn a lifetime of repressed feeling. He believed that this would require some professional help.

Phil's goals hadn't changed. He still wanted to have satisfying friendships and be able to be more comfortable with women. If he hadn't recognised the sometimes desperate feelings of isolation and loneliness that his speech impediment had caused him, he suspected that he might never have acknowledged possibilities his life now held for closeness.

Kate's issue was whether she could combine her career with having a partner and being a mother. She realised that if the time came for her to make such a choice, she would be able to do so. For the present, however, she could see that she needed to concentrate on changing her attitudes and her lifestyle so that she could enhance the possibility of meeting a potential partner.

Julie now felt more confident about the steps she was taking towards being successfully independent. She realised the importance of not taking things for granted and that although she could make conscious choices, the decisions she made had consequences. She would need to think about these as she planned ahead.

As a result of the seminar, Moira had extended her life-line off the page. Despite what anyone else might think, she believed she still had a lot of living to do. Her aim was to plan for a full and happy retirement.

DO YOU WANT TO MAKE SOME CHANGES IN THE WAY YOU LIVE YOUR LIFE SO THAT YOU CAN ASSERT YOUR OWN NEEDS AND WANTS MORE?

If so, now is the time to plan for the life you would like to create from this day on. Before moving on, however, write your responses to the final exercise, remembering that you can return whenever you wish to revise or change your plans as you progress through the days, months and years ahead. So as you bear in mind that life is a process and that you have the right to change, ask yourself:

WHAT STEPS DO I WANT TO TAKE TO DEVELOP AND MAKE MORE OF MY SINGLE LIFESTYLE?

MY LONGTERM GOALS?

MY SHORT-TERM GOALS?

MY FIRST STEPS?

# 3

Some singular
issues

# RESPONSIBILITY FOR SELF

*I*f you have completed your workbook exercises and have given serious heed to the various ways that the seminar participants responded, you no doubt realise that there is no one right way of answering the challenges that confront the single person. And with this comes an awareness of some of the active steps you can take now and in the near future to live your life more to your satisfaction. You know that you have the power to make decisions and to act upon them – that you need not be dependent.

As a single person you have a tremendous range of life options to choose from because you have fewer responsi bilities that are to do with a partner and a shared lifestyle. Yet this freedom of choice can be onerous and is avoided by those who prefer to be dependent or who have little sense of their own potency and their ability to take charge of their lives.

## Finding inner security

Remember that it is up to you and no one else to ensure that your physical, material and emotional needs are met. You can balance your lifestyle so that you have a healthy blend of work, social and physical activities. You are responsible for writing your own recipe for growth through the pursuit and attainment of goals you set yourself. You have a fund of creative energy within you that seeks expression. It is up to you to discover the outlets that bring you most pleasure. You have a spiritual self that is committed to finding purpose and meaning in your existence and this requires effort on your part.

Unless you can embrace the concept of responsibility wholeheartedly it is unlikely that you will ever have a strong sense of security and stability, regardless of whether you are single or in a partnership. No one else can provide you with this gift no matter how much they love and care for you. As you read through the various issues raised in this section, remind yourself of the importance of loving yourself and of the power you have within you to manage the challenges you experience in your single life.

## Growth to the end

Essential to anything I say about being single is my belief that we all have the power within us to develop our potentiality until the day we die.

As we have seen, our conditioning influences the way we develop. Like flowers we thrive and blossom when we have the opportunity to grow in a nourishing and supportive environment. Yet we differ from plants in that if our early experiences were in barren soil and stunting of growth, we have the power as adults to remove ourselves to a more fertile environment and to consciously seek to enrich our lives by adding the elements we need in order for us to prosper.

# Loneliness

Loneliness is regarded as something of a dirty word in our society. Many people think there is something terribly wrong with them if they reach the point of acknowledging their loneliness. Yet loneliness can be a positive emotion in that it is a statement of an unfulfilled desire to share and as such can propel us into taking constructive steps towards happiness. It is easy to avoid recognising things that we would prefer not to face; feelings of loneliness are often ignored, to the detriment of our well-being.

Dr James Lynch, in his trail-blazing book, *The Broken Heart, The Medical Consequences of Loneliness* points out that it is far more acceptable to have the physical symptoms that can result from loneliness – heart disease, cancer, blood pressure and the like – than it is to acknowledge their underlying cause. We have medical centres and foundations for most physical diseases but nowhere do we find an institute for the welfare of 'the heart'.

Maybe you see yourself as unfortunately lonely because you don't have a particular person to share your life. If so, it is important to realise that before someone can be the special person in your life you need to be able to offer them true friendship. Many people who are desperately seeking a mate fail to recognise or avail themselves of the opportunities for friendship and happiness that abound in life.

Investing large amounts of time and energy in work or frenetic activity can indicate that you are running away from admitting to yourself that you are not happy and, quite likely, lonely. Crowding the hours of your day with things you 'have to do' or with people you 'have to see' can do little to fill the void you may not dare to recognise. Until you can stop and acknowledge these unsatisfied feelings, you will not find contentment or be able to open your heart to the love you have to give, let alone the love you so want to receive.

Do you find it difficult to just stop, and be with yourself and listen to the messages that your body and your heart have to say to you? If so, it is likely that you have problems valuing yourself. There is so much wisdom within you if you care to take the time and make the effort to heed it. I have seen dramatic changes take place in people who have taken up conscious relaxation techniques, meditation or Tai Chi as a means of tuning themselves into their bodies, minds and emotions.

Once loneliness is acknowledged, then what?

It takes courage to reach out and express the desire to share more intimately with people or a person. If you feel that you lack the confidence or social skills required, it could be a good idea for you to investigate courses on developing communication skills, self-assertion or self-confidence. It may also be worthwhile inquiring about public speaking groups or acting classes as these can serve a two-fold purpose. Not only do they help to build skills in communication and self-expression, they also provide opportunities for mixing socially and learning to listen to others.

If you believe that you have serious blocks within yourself that prevent you from initiating social contact and making close friendships don't hesitate to see a counsellor or psychologist. There is no need to suffer unnecessarily when there are people with the skills to assist you to bring more happiness into your life.

Sharing common interests is an enjoyable way of making an initial connection with people because you have something to do and to talk about from the start. It is up to you to make the effort to choose an activity or pastime that you would like to pursue and then to take the steps to do so. If you are prepared to become actively involved in an interest or activity group rather than in being a bystander, inevitably you will find people with whom you would like to share more of yourself, people who have the potential to be your friends.

A rewarding way of meeting new and interesting people (and of giving similar satisfaction to others) is through networking. For much of my life I have enjoyed introducing people who share something in common – be this an interest, a nationality, a business idea, an approach to life or whatever. By inviting such people into my home or setting up a meeting in a restaurant or public place I have often had the pleasure of seeing supportive contacts made, many of which have then developed into close friendships. On several occasions through such a 'network' I have also been introduced to people who now number among those who are most important in my life. It is a wonderful way of giving and receiving.

Who do you know that someone else would like to know? Do something about it!

# Shyness

Being shy or introverted can be an obstacle to people making contact at a comfortable and meaningful level, especially in situations that are unfamiliar and which leave little opportunity for quiet conversation. However, while ways of meeting seem to be more restricted for them, introverted people must realise that there is nothing wrong with being quiet or introspective or shy. Being reserved can be an attractive quality. Indeed, I have met many men and women who would prefer to share their time and leisure with someone who is not interested in being the life of the party.

If you are a shy person don't try to battle with the noise and bustle that is characteristic of so many singles bars and meeting places. It is often less stressful and more congenial to ask small groups of people to visit you at home. Entertaining need not be a grand affair. If you have met people you'd like to know better, why not ask them onto 'your territory' where you feel confident? A glass of wine and cheese, or coffee and pastries are enough to fill the spaces that arise in any conversation.

Many shy people are afraid that once they commit themselves by showing they are interested in getting to know someone, they will be rejected. This is a common fear, and one sometimes given great weight through bitter experience. What shy people tend to overlook is that in life, it would be fair to say that 50 per cent of the times you reach out to others you may not get the positive response you hoped for, yet on the other 50 per cent you will. This ratio probably applies equally to the extrovert and to the introvert. However, the extrovert copes better and doesn't let us see how the rebuff hurts.

The law of averages is the basis of the 50/50 split. In fact I would say the chances of being rebuffed are far less than that, particularly if your approach is friendly and open. The point is, that fear of what may happen is a great handicap. It prevents you from finding others to whom you can relate. Risk the rebuff; the potential of finding a friend goes far beyond the temporary dent to your ego that 'may' eventuate if you reach out to others without success on a particular occasion.

If you are reserved it may require a little extra effort on your part to make your interest in having friendships and close relationships known and appreciated. Just remember that the responsibility for taking steps towards initiating happiness for yourself rests largely with you.

# Living singly together

Often single people are isolated by where they live. You don't have to be the sole inhabitant of a country property to be geographically disadvantaged as far as sharing with others is concerned. You can feel isolated in a house in sprawling suburbia. This sort of isolation is common among those who are single again and who remain living in what was their family home. Occupying an apartment can be equally isolating given the anonymity and lack of common living space of such multi-storey residential buildings.

These days it is totally acceptable for single people to share accommodation. Given the cost of housing it is regarded as a sensible way of finding pleasant living circumstances on a single income. More importantly such shared accommodation makes it possible to ensure that there is company, especially if you do not like to go home to an empty place. Sharing a house or flat also provides opportunities for learning the give and take that living together entails. If you choose your housemates on the basis of likely compatibility of interests, attitudes and preferred lifestyle, you'll enhance your chances of developing real friendship and understanding.

An advantage that comes from such sharing is that you can meet the friends of those you live with and in this way increase your own circle of acquaintances and friends. If you are interested in finding shared accommodation, newspapers usually have a 'to share' column. Noticeboards at colleges, universities or at the corner store in an area in which you would like to live are also good places to look or to advertise. There are even professionally monitored businesses that specialise in assisting people to find congenial shared accommodation.

Living in a communal household where the occupants vary widely in age, and where some are coupled and have children, has many positive aspects. It provides companionship and its members can benefit from having an extended family. Children in such a household can learn from a variety of adults. They do not need to be so reliant upon one or two parents for the development of their personalities. For single parents, the opportunity to have adult company at hand and to, perhaps, share some of the emotional responsibility for the children, is supportive.

The joining of two or more single parent households can be a boon for the adults and a rich learning experience for children. At a time when children may suffer from the breakdown of their web of security after a divorce or separation, the presence of others who have been through the same experience creates special bonds. In these cases, too, the economic benefits of pooling resources cannot be overlooked.

It is a pity that the option of asking an older person to join a communal household does not have wider acceptance. The selection process requires open eyes on both sides, an open acknowledgment of the generation gap, and a freedom to speak up. Of course, there is danger of an older person becoming an unwilling babysitter or being taken for granted, but on the beneficial side is the pleasure of being an active part of a communal 'family'.

Single men and women in a communal situation can have a lot of their needs for friendship and intimacy met. They are also not isolated from children as is often the case for the person without a partner or a family. They have the advantage of sharing the everyday domestic chores as well, and taking on something of the responsibility that comes with living with others.

A 'couple' I know who share a lovely home are in fact singles. He is gay and she is very definitely heterosexual. For both of them their shared household is an ideal resolution of their desire to live singly yet together.

# SINGLE AND SEXUAL

*M*any of today's myths and images of what it is to be a single person revolve around sexuality. It seems that the unattached person either has a feast or a famine of sex depending on who is telling the story.

As you explore what being single and sexual means to you I would like to point out that regardless of whether or not you lead a sexually active life, you are a sexual being and your sexuality is something to recognise, value, and express.

Remember, too, that being sexual does not mean 'having sex'. While to some people sexuality is equated with sheer lust, this does not necessarily have to be the case. I have met men and women who exude an almost palpable energy that could be deemed sexual, yet who do not engage in any sexual activity as such, be this through choice or circumstance.

We are born with a sexual energy that is with us until the day we die. To suppress this life force is to suppress our creativity, our personality, our sensuality, to dampen the vitality we emanate that attracts people to us and helps give our life meaning. When I ask you to enjoy expressing this energy within you it is important to realise that I'm talking about being 'sexual', not 'sexy', though there's nothing wrong with the latter if you are prepared to take responsibility for the consequences.

## Some practicalities . . .

In the 1980s it is generally accepted, even if not approved, that people will have sexual liaisons and relationships without being married. It is also quite commonly assumed that a single person is likely to enjoy a number of sex partners. Yet I dare to suggest that for the majority of the unattached, being single and sexual today is not smooth sailing.

For single men and women who are not comfortable with the more free and easy attitudes to casual sex that have been prevalent since the advent of the contraceptive pill, the satisfaction of their sexual needs can be a real issue. Even for those who are not averse to sex without commitment, it is not necessarily easy to feel sexually satisfied. From my discussions with many liberated singles, I know that it can be difficult to find compatible bedmates and that even if they do, sex in itself does not give most of them the fulfilment that they are seeking.

I do not want to promote a particular moral stance as I ask you to think about the role sexuality plays in your own life. I believe it is up to you to act responsibly as an adult and to consider the values that are important to you in your relationships with other people, determining for yourself what you regard as acceptable behaviour. In working out your guidelines be aware that people who are potential sex partners may hold different attitudes and expectations about what 'having sex' means.

It is very much up to you to be responsible for letting someone who is interested in having a sexual relationship with you know where you stand. You may need to assert what is important to you if disappointment and misunderstanding is not to occur. This is not always easy. At times we are not readily heard. . .

As I write I have a clear picture of a beautiful Malaysian-Indian woman of 34 who attended one of my seminars, entitled 'Being Single and Sexual'. During our discussion it became apparent that she had been feeling quite depressed because she had concluded that to be acceptable to men she would have to change her values and her moral code – or mask her appearance and her personality so that she would not be noticed.

It seemed a tragedy that this woman, who loved to look and feel good, who enjoyed dressing well and making the most of her appearance, and whose personality was a magnet to most people she met, felt that she would either have to become a recluse or dress dowdily and look ugly if she were to be able to maintain the high principles concerning sexual practice that were her cultural and religious heritage.

As we talked it seemed that her problem was not in fact so much one of her attractiveness being misread as a come on by the men she encountered but rather more the difficulty she had telling any man who expressed interest in her that, while she was indeed 'sexual', she was not available for casual affairs. It was not until she found herself in potentially compromising situations that she would say that she was not interested in casual sex because her convictions required that she be a virgin when she married. Unintentionally she gave mixed messages. She left it to almost the last moment to say 'no', and it was not surprising that men were disappointed and she did not hear from them again.

After the seminar she realised that she could express her moral stance and still have men date her. The difficulty she'd had communicating her viewpoint to men she met socially virtually disappeared. Asserting early on what was important to her made all the difference. The men who then chose to share her company did so on her terms.

Assuming responsibility for letting a potential sex partner know what our attitudes towards a sexual relationship are can be difficult. Yet so much unnecessary distress can result when two people who have very different needs and expectations spend sexual time together without voicing expectations that I think it is usually well worth the effort – and potential embarrassment – of speaking our mind. Casual sex is comfortable and fun for some people but for others sharing a bed still signifies something serious and ongoing.

Sexual responsibility has another aspect; it entails ensuring that there is no possibility of an unwanted pregnancy, nor the spread of sexually transmitted diseases that are so prevalent at the present time.

Sexually active singles need to be very responsible about protecting themselves, and their partners, if they have more than one sexual relationship, from contagious diseases. The AIDS virus has been so effective in arousing fear among those whose lifestyle has been sexually promiscuous that many have changed their sexual practices, some to the extreme of choosing to be celibate. Even men and women who have always been very discriminating about their choice of sex partners are wary and it is not unusual to hear such singles say that they no longer think that sex is worth the risks involved.

## A sexual scale

Consider the following rating scale. If you are not in a sexual relationship imagine that you are. Regardless of how important sex is to you, as you rate your responses you will gain some insights into yourself and your sexuality that may help you to enjoy and appreciate your life and your friendships more.

| | CIRCLE THE MOST APPROPRIATE RATING |
|---|---|
| TO GIVE AFFECTION | 1 2 3 4 5 6 7 8 9 10<br>NOT AT ALL        VERY MUCH |
| TO SURRENDER MYSELF TO ANOTHER | 1 2 3 4 5 6 7 8 9 10 |
| TO BE HELD CLOSE | 1 2 3 4 5 6 7 8 9 10 |
| TO FEEL SOMEHOW 'WHOLE' | 1 2 3 4 5 6 7 8 9 10 |
| TO FEEL ATTRACTIVE/ DESIRABLE | 1 2 3 4 5 6 7 8 9 10 |
| TO RELEASE PENT-UP ENERGY | 1 2 3 4 5 6 7 8 9 10 |
| TO HAVE COMPANIONSHIP | 1 2 3 4 5 6 7 8 9 10 |

| | |
|---|---|
| TO SHOW MY LOVE | 1 2 3 4 5 6 7 8 9 10 |
| TO 'LOSE MYSELF' | 1 2 3 4 5 6 7 8 9 10 |
| TO FEEL LOVED | 1 2 3 4 5 6 7 8 9 10 |
| TO COMMUNICATE INTIMATELY | 1 2 3 4 5 6 7 8 9 10 |
| TO RECEIVE WARMTH | 1 2 3 4 5 6 7 8 9 10 |
| TO FEEL CONNECTED WITH SOMEONE ELSE | 1 2 3 4 5 6 7 8 9 10 |
| TO EXPRESS MY POWER | 1 2 3 4 5 6 7 8 9 10 |
| TO FONDLE AND CARESS | 1 2 3 4 5 6 7 8 9 10 |
| TO BE TOUCHED | 1 2 3 4 5 6 7 8 9 10 |
| TO 'LET MYSELF GO' | 1 2 3 4 5 6 7 8 9 10 |
| TO PROVE MY SEXUALITY | 1 2 3 4 5 6 7 8 9 10 |
| TO HAVE ORGASMS | 1 2 3 4 5 6 7 8 9 10 |
| TO HOLD SOMEONE CLOSE | 1 2 3 4 5 6 7 8 9 10 |
| TO GIVE PLEASURE TO SOMEONE ELSE | 1 2 3 4 5 6 7 8 9 10 |
| TO BE KISSED AND CUDDLED | 1 2 3 4 5 6 7 8 9 10 |
| TO FEEL SECURE IN A RELATIONSHIP | 1 2 3 4 5 6 7 8 9 10 |
| TO SHOW MY COMMITMENT | 1 2 3 4 5 6 7 8 9 10 |
| TO BE SEXUALLY EXCITED | 1 2 3 4 5 6 7 8 9 10 |
| TO FEEL SELF-CONFIDENT | 1 2 3 4 5 6 7 8 9 10 |
| TO HAVE A SENSE OF BELONGING | 1 2 3 4 5 6 7 8 9 10 |

As you look at your responses it is interesting to note whether your needs or desires are more active than passive. Do you want to give more than to receive or vice-versa? Each of us varies in the degree to which we give or receive. However, if there is to be a real sharing between two people, be this between lovers or virtual strangers, there usually needs to be a balance between give and take. The more both partners experience the satisfaction of giving and receiving, the more likely their being together will be enjoyable. This principle applies not only to sharing sex but also to most personal communication between two people.

Can you see from your responses whether your sexual satisfactions are more physical, emotional or psychological? Is sharing with someone sexually for you a sensual excitement and release, or is it an opportunity to express and receive feelings like affection and love? Or are your greatest needs to do with security, commitment and belonging?

Because there are so many different needs that we may want to express or have satisfied in a sexual relationship, it is no wonder that casual sex can be disappointing, especially if our underlying desire is to feel loved and secure. Letting another person know what we want in our sexual sharing requires trust and the desire of both people to understand and strive to give their partner pleasure. This can be difficult to express, even for two people who know each other well. Our needs can also vary according to time and circumstance which complicates things further.

Our gender can also influence our approach to sex. Women and men have traditionally been seen to differ in their attitudes – men being more concerned with lust while for women sexual intercourse is more a statement of love. There would seem to be some truth in this perceived variation between the sexes, though it is debatable whether it is biologically determined or more a result of conditioning. I suspect that as many men as women yearn for the intimacy possible while making love.

## Sex with strangers

These days with women's liberation and the increased acceptance of sex without commitment, women and men are more openly available for casual sex. Whether you are male or female, if you are a single person who has one night stands it is impossible for you to expect these encounters to satisfy your deeper needs. If you accept this before you have casual sex, your expectations are likely to be realistic and your enjoyment of the experience far greater.

Many people who see themselves as single have one or more regular sex partners. These relationships are far more likely to satisfy their needs for warmth, friendship, intimate communication and security than the fleeting affair. As long as both people hold similar expectations of their relationship, sharing sexually yet living singly can be a congenial and satisfactory resolution to the dilemma of maintaining independence, while gaining the advantages that having a sexual companion provide.

Unfortunately, often the different needs that such sex partners have means that they hold different expectations. A sad example of this can occur when a single woman has an ongoing relationship with a married man. In such instances her unacknowledged desire for commitment may cause her to fantasise about her lover leaving his spouse and family for her at some time in the not too distant future. Perhaps he might. Yet such expectations if they remain unspoken can lead to pain and disappointment.

I have met women who have remained enmeshed in an affair with a married man for a decade or more hoping against hope that the man will eventually start a new life and family with her. It is tragic when a woman in this situation realises that she is getting beyond childbearing years and sees the futility of her longheld unrealistic expectations.

## Finding satisfaction

Before closing this discussion of being single and sexual, look through your responses to the rating scale again. Can you see ways of expressing or satisfying any of these desires and needs other than through being with someone sexually?

When I responded to this question for the first time I was quite surprised to realise that I could have all of these needs and wants met to varying degrees without being in a sexual relationship. At the time I had been feeling very sorry for myself because a serious love affair had come to an end. To realise that I did not have to be dependent on my lover for the satisfaction of many of my needs helped me to see alternatives I'd forgotten in my unhappiness. While it was difficult to accept that I could no longer rely on our relationship and sexual sharing as my primary source of contentment, I could see that there was nothing to stop me finding fulfilment in other ways. Once again I appreciated my close, intimate friendships.

# Single and gay

I do not want to say much about the nature of gay sexual relationships as my experience is limited because I am heterosexual. Yet from the many discussions I have had with homosexual men and women over the years, I believe that most of what I have said in *Successfully Single* is relevant to all single men and women, regardless of their sexual preferences. The lifestyle of a homosexual person is likely to differ in some fundamental respects from that of the heterosexual, but I see no evidence to indicate that as far as the deeper needs for warmth, love, acceptance, recognition and personal growth are concerned there is any obvious difference. The ways to finding satisfaction may well vary but the underlying motivation is the same.

## Male and gay

If they actively participate in a permissive gay lifestyle, gay men need to be able to separate the physical aspects of their sexual needs from the emotional needs for a relationship. Given the nature of the gay scene, this is not always easy. The heavy emphasis placed upon appearance, youth and glamour and the frequently felt pressure to attract numerous sex partners can make it difficult for many a gay man who wants to be successfully single.

To have a strong sense of self-confidence and self-worth is likely to be very hard at times if you are a male and homosexual. Not only do you have to assert your own sexual preference and lifestyle in a society where to be gay is often still considered abnormal and unacceptable, but you also need to question the assumptions and the 'hype' that pressure you to conform to the 'scene'.

It can take courage to ask yourself whether you need to go along with the images presented in camp magazines or to query the expectations that may prevail in gay bars and discos and among your friends and acquaintances. To be single is the norm for the gay person yet the lifestyle portrayed as ideal is likely to cause disillusion and disappointment unless the purely physical and transient models for sexual satisfaction are seen for what they are.

I have heard many homosexual men admit that what they are really looking for is a relationship in which they feel loved and appreciated for who they are rather than what they look like. Their desire is no different to that expressed by the majority of heterosexual people. Neither is the response I give. My recommendation to anyone who wants to be valued for their own unique individuality is that they focus their energy on developing their potentiality to be interesting and attractive to themselves and to others in dimensions that are not purely superficial.

Just as for anyone who is single, the gay person is responsible for their own happiness . . . and for the implications that their behaviour may hold for others in their life. It almost goes without saying that, more than ever before, the sexually active gay male needs to take particular precaution against sexually transmitted diseases. The alarmingly high rate of death that has resulted from the spreading of the AIDS virus has served as a brake on the more promiscuous practices that have been regarded as part and parcel of 'normal' gay life.

Without wishing to moralise I would suggest that if you are a homosexual male you seriously think about your values, about what is important to you in your life and relationships and the sort of sex you find most satisfying. If you want to take risks make sure they are well calculated, that you protect yourself as far as possible, and that you are prepared to wear the consequences.

The happiest men who are gay that I have met are those who, like any successfully single person, have a strong sense of themselves, who have a sense of purpose and direction, who have some rich friendships and who are interested and challenged by life and relationships. They are men who accept their sexuality and are not embarrassed to declare their preference; they see it as a part of themselves rather than as something that sets them apart. One man's way of developing a very satisfying and rewarding lifestyle which reflects and expresses his homosexuality is included in the interviews in Part Four of this book.

# . . . and what about women who are gay?

I have intentionally differentiated between the issues that confront homosexual men and women. Generally speaking gay women are more concerned with the quality of their relationships than they are with the physical enjoyment of casual or multiple sexual encounters.

Some years ago I met an American woman whose story illustrates various differences I perceive between men and women who have a homosexual preference and, in some salient ways, differences that I also see occurring between men and women in society at large that cause confusion and misunderstanding.

It was not until she was in her mid-thirties that Mary chose to have lesbian relationships. Like most women, she had grown up assuming that she would date men and eventually marry one who would then be her sex partner for life. True to this scenario she married Pete when they finished their studies, as he had been the man in her life since she was nineteen. After less than three years he left her on the grounds of irreconcilable differences. Some years later she married Joe only to find that the same problems in communication came up. This time she brought the marriage to an end.

I was initially somewhat surprised that Mary had consciously chosen to be lesbian. Clearly she had enjoyed sex with men and did not believe that she had always had latent lesbian tendencies. In fact she said that it was not until the ending of her second marriage that she had even thought about women being attractive to her in the sexual sense. It had taken time and considerable mental effort for her to see women as potential sex partners.

So why choose women?

As Mary sees things, it was a logical step for her to take. Although she enjoyed sex and shared interests with both her male partners, she had been dissatisfied. She had not felt that she could communicate at the level of intimacy she had wanted to with either man. Both husbands were reluctant to let her explore issues that were important to her – a problem she had never known in the close friendships she'd had with women.

Although she really enjoyed her sexuality and sensuality, Mary wanted intimate friendship as well as a bed partner. One day, after talking frankly about her dilemma with an old college friend who was a lesbian, she started to think whether 'to love women' could be a viable alternative for her. To extend the intimacy she had always known with her close female friends to include sexual communication made sense. As she sees it now, choosing to love women in the total sense is a solution to satisfying the expectations she held of relationships.

Although not easy to go against the conditioning she'd had since childhood, Mary now finds women to be immensely attractive to her. Since her divorce three years ago she has shared a house with another woman. Their relationship is not an exclusive one, yet the warm, caring communication they have had for many a year now extends quite naturally to sharing a bed.

If you are a woman who is gay, it is likely that you have a network of friends who you can turn to for support, encouragement and love. To be successfully single and successfully yourself it is important that you know and express your own values and live in accordance with these. It is easy to become involved in role play, to pretend to be what you are not so that you fit the expectations of the people who are close to you. Remember that your sexual preference is but a part of you and that you do not have to play a particular part.

# THE ISSUE OF ISSUE

*F*or many singles, especially women who are in their thirties, an important dilemma they face is whether or not to have children. For those who have always wanted to do so and have assumed that they would, this issue can cause great consternation and distress as the end of their child-bearing years looms near.

These days it is not uncommon for women who seriously desire to have a child, and see no immediate prospect of meeting a mate, or prefer not to have a particular partner, or are lesbian, to deliberately become pregnant and have a child on their own. Although such a decision is essentially a personal rather than a moral one, on a practical level I would emphasise the tremendous responsibility a woman has in this situation. She must understand her motives and seriously consider the implications this choice has for her own life and, more importantly, that of the child.

If you are a woman for whom this decision is critical, I recommend you read a book entitled *Why Children?* edited by Stephanie Dowrick.

Obviously the decision to have a child on one's own presupposes a maturity, a stability and an ability to manage tremendous stress, far more than is usually required of a woman who has the support and love of a partner. It also presumes the ability to provide the material wherewithal for you and your child.

Something that women in this dilemma also need to heed are the feelings of the man who is involved in the conception of the planned child. Several questions need to be asked. Does the father have paternity rights? If not, why not? Should he be told of the planned pregnancy? Should he be told he is a parent? Should the child know the identity of its father?

The Australian census statistics for 1981 indicate that the decision to have a child on their own is not common to the majority of single women. Yet for those who love children and who regard being childless a sore source of disappointment in their lives, it can be difficult to see alternative ways of satisfying their maternal needs.

If you are a woman or a man who would love to have children of your own and haven't, you don't have to look far to see that there are many children in this world who are in need of your love and affection. There are also many mothers who would appreciate sharing the responsibility of raising their youngsters.

Giving is the best route to receiving. Whether it is through fostering a desperately needy child in an undeveloped country, being a real or pretend aunt or uncle, babysitting for your friends, or 'adopting' a child who is confined to living in hospital, the possibilities for delight in helping children to blossom in this world are there for you.

# Single and a parent

I do not want to suggest how you might best go about parenting effectively as a person without a partner. There are many books on that subject by people with far more expertise than I have. Instead, it is my intention to explore some of the issues that confront the single parent as they strive to have their own needs satisfied as well as those of their children.

Any self-respecting single parent should be prepared to regard their own requirements as of high priority and seek to satisfy them as best they can for their family's well-being as well as their own. But to acknowledge this can be hard for many single parents, especially when they feel responsible and guilty for the ending of a relationship that has resulted in their offspring being one parent less. Such self-blame undermines self-respect and happiness and does not add an iota of joy to a child's life.

Unless we respect and value ourselves, how can we expect a child to either?

If you find it difficult to recognise your own worth, even after completing the self-awareness exercises earlier in the book, I recommend you seek professional assistance. You are worth it!

Once you recognise your needs and acknowledge your right to have these met, it is up to you to take the necessary steps. These usually require organisation on your part and a sharing of responsibility. If you are certain, for example, that you want to take an evening or two off to do something you feel of value to your well-being, you will find people who will assist you. Ask for help. It may be a case of reciprocating in kind or perhaps paying someone to help mind the children. Often grandparents are only waiting to be asked! If you are determined to do something for yourself, the solution will emerge.

## Overcoming isolation

Often a mother or father who has primary custody of her or his children voices how alone they feel. Despite being constantly occupied with domestic responsibilities they long for the companionship and stimulation of adult company. No matter how delightful they find the contact and communication they have with a child, they cannot expect the sort of satisfactions they gain from sharing with someone who is mature. Also, although they help to fill a void, television and talk-back radio are no real substitute for the live companionship of another person.

Given the responsibility a parent has to ensure that a child is being competently and caringly looked after, especially in the early years, it is not surprising that many a single parent feels house-bound. The problem is often exacerbated for those who live in suburbs where houses are set on largish blocks in streets that are at car rather than walking distance from shops and easy access to other people, especially other single people. The suburban two-parent milieu can be insensitive to the needs of the single parent after divorce, death or separation. Help and warmth may not be forthcoming if the single parent is seen as potentially threatening to their way of life or their relationship.

If you feel you are living in isolated circumstances consider moving your family to an area where you would have more ready access to adult company, to a convenient shopping centre and to child-care. Or consider sharing your home with another single person, perhaps someone who like yourself has children. Not only does this resolve the adult company problem, but it also can help to reduce the costs of living which can be crippling for a parent trying to manage on their own.

The fact that you have a built-in babysitter can also be of tremendous value.

There are a number of organisations that aim to provide social interaction for their members. One such organisation is Parents Without Partners. Not only do they organise functions and activities, many of which are open to children, but they also offer emotional support because all of those who belong know what it is like to be single and a parent. Once you know several people who are in a similar situation to yourself you can then help each other.

Perhaps you would prefer not to seek companionship through an organisation, in which case there are plenty of informal opportunities for meeting congenial people in the community around you. One enterprising mother with four children under the age of seven took a practical step. She put up a sign on the local primary school noticeboard inviting any other single parent to share childminding and take turns with shopping. She had more than a score of responses which is not surprising given that at many schools the number of children from single parent families is well over the 50 per cent mark. Not only has this circle helped to relieve some of the pressures of day-to-day life for a housebound single parent but it has also opened a network for support and friendship.

Also, don't forget that the married couples in your area or among your friends may well be an important resource for you. Not only are they likely to welcome your invitations to drop-in or be pleased to take you along when they go shopping, but they might also be really happy to do some child-minding, particularly if their own children have grown up or if they are childless.

All too often we hesitate to reach out to others for fear of being a burden when in fact by doing so we can add to the pleasure that they have in life.

## What about sex?

There is no doubt that being responsible for raising a family single-handed can limit opportunities for meeting people. To meet 'someone special' and then develop a sexual relationship can seem an impossibility.

Like any other person who is single, the responsibility for organising your life to maximise the opportunities for satisfying your needs is your own. Have you considered joining a singles' interest group or social club or an association for single parents like Parents Without Partners? Or a reputable introduction agency? For some people advertising in the personal columns has been a successful way of meeting people who are happy to accept that they have children.

From my discussions with many people who are parenting solo I know that problems arise when a promising relationship begins to develop. Never far from a single parent's mind is: what will the kids think?

While it is obviously very important to be sensitive to your children's needs you should not allow your own happiness to be over-ruled by their perceptions of how having other people in your life might affect them. Bear in mind that they are young, that they do not really understand your needs and that any fears that they have about their relationship with you being jeopardised by a stranger make sense. This is particularly likely to be the case if they have been involved in the trauma that often surrounds the ending of an unhappy marriage. It is important that you give them your reassurance and love, yet at the same time be clear that you will not allow their anxieties to unreasonably govern your life.

It is not unusual to hear that a single parent has not been out on a date since his or her marriage ended a dozen or more years beforehand because the children didn't want them too. Like many a good parent, they put what they thought to be the children's best interests before their own. It is sad when later they realise that they probably have been martyrs unnecessarily. The chances of starting a new life and relationship are often slimmer for those in the middle years of life.

If you do want to have an active social and sex life, I think it is in both you and your children's best interests to do so. However, there are some questions that as a single parent you need to ask yourself.

When should I let the children know that I'm dating with romance in view?

For those who have very warm and open communication with their family, the answer more often than not is that they want to share with them from the outset the excitement and the anxiety they may feel when meeting someone new. Whenever possible such single parents try to arrange things so that the person being met is also introduced to the children, so that they feel included in the exciting venture.

For many parents, however, the idea of exposing their children to a number of different strangers is seen as negative and potentially distressing for all concerned. In such instances they arrange to meet away from home. Only if a serious relationship develops do they choose to introduce their friend to their brood.

Whatever decision you make about such an issue will depend upon your own values, the way you communicate with your children and how secure and confident they are in your love.

Dilemmas can also arise when you decide you want to spend sexual time with a friend. Do you have them stay overnight in your home or do you ensure that your meetings are away from prying eyes? Only you can determine what is the best thing to do, taking into consideration your own attitudes and values and the impact that your behaviour is likely to have on your children.

# A mother/father figure for my kids?

For single parents who do not have an 'ex' that the children spend time with, a problem that often arises is: how can I teach my child the things that they would learn from a parent of the opposite sex? Many people have consciously addressed this issue and come up with novel solutions and effective results.

The outcome of one blind date was a platonic friendship that came to have great benefit for a woman's young son. She now regards it as one of the best things that has happened. When she saw that her youngster had taken a liking to her friend after he had visited their home on a couple of occasions, she thought that he could perhaps help her by becoming an 'adopted uncle'. To her relief he was delighted by her request and has since been there when needed as a father figure and friend.

A businessman whose wife left him with custody of their two daughters was faced with the problem of how best to raise them while he also met the commitments of his small and struggling company. He was reluctant to have a variety of baby-sitters to look after them and he could not afford a full-time nanny. He successfully resolved his dilemma by advertising for a single mother who would do light domestic duties and care for his children in return for accommodation and a small income. His daughters responded well to their 'surrogate mum' and her own child gained a father figure and a family too.

# SINGLE AGAIN

*T*here are many men and women who are unhappily single because they have not been able to come to terms with the ending of their marriage. They believe that they have failed. Yet for whatever reason a relationship breaks up, it is tragic for both or either of the partners to feel that they have had their chance and that they have 'blown it'. Some believe that their life is to be lonely and unhappy forever, almost as punishment for their not having succeeded. Unfortunately many people today belong to the ranks of the walking wounded.

There is no doubt that one of the greatest challenges that can result from being single again is how to overcome feelings of inadequacy and the loss of direction and purpose in life. Unless we are prepared to use this negative experience constructively it can be extremely difficult to regain our feelings of self-confidence and self-worth.

The process of regaining self-confidence and a positive attitude to what the future holds can take time and demand a preparedness to do some soul-searching. This period of reappraisal is one of tremendous potential for growth. It is an opportunity to learn from past experiences so that conscious decisions can be made to find fulfilment in the new phase ahead.

Creative ways of living happily together without a partner can result from sharing experiences with others who are also single again. Ken's story illustrates how one man who sank to the depths of depression and self-recrimination when his marriage ended was able to rediscover his self-worth and the possibilities for happiness his future held through such sharing.

I met Ken only once, when he came to one of my seminars, Being Single Again. He was obviously tense. The way his clothes hung on his frame suggested that he had lost a lot of weight. His face was drawn and throughout most of the day it was quite devoid of expression, as if there were no spirit inside him. When the seminar ended I was concerned that his expectations had perhaps not been met.

I was delighted, therefore, some months later to receive this letter from him which told of how stopping and thinking about himself and his past in a constructive way and listening to the experiences of others had helped him to find a positive path through his pain and to move forward towards his future.

Dear Yvonne,

I don't know that you will remember me but I was at your Single Again seminar last May. While I didn't say very much during the day, I want you to know it was a turning point in my life.

As I said at the seminar, my marriage came to an abrupt end in October last year. What I didn't say was that I had reached such depths of hurt, self-doubt and despair that I was considering not going on.

When Judith and the kids left me I felt shattered. In my saner moments I knew neither of us was particularly to blame. Yet questions kept continually running around my head like: 'Where did I go wrong?' 'What's wrong with me?'.

At the time the only conclusion I could come to was that it was all my fault.

I just went through the motions of each day like some

sort of robot. At times I would say to myself 'this is the end – I'm finished'.

I spent day after day aimlessly, criticising myself, trying to understand what had happened. Sometimes I would start dialling the number of someone I know only to stop before the last digit. I just couldn't make contact with friends or acquaintances . . . and I would cut off any attempts from my family to help me with a casual 'I'm OK'. I was too embarrassed to ask for, or accept, help.

I started going to singles bars. I started to chase sex for the sake of it, maybe to prove myself. But there was no satisfaction in waking up with a throbbing head and vague memories of being in a bed with someone, somewhere. I felt even more frustrated because now not only was I a failure but I disliked myself for what I was doing. My doubts about my ability to meet and cope with women increased. When I next found myself in bed with a woman I was impotent.

I stopped going to the bars. Sitting at home each night I'd drink until the early hours of the morning, trying to stop my mind, boozing myself to sleep. Masturbation helped. I bought porn movies and magazines but my interest in these became so consuming that I felt somehow perverted. I was disgusted with myself.

The way out for me started that day at the seminar when I realised that other people were in similar situations – and worse.

Focusing that day on my strengths instead of all the weaknesses helped me to pull myself together. I remembered what you said about getting the energy going, about doing. When I thought about the exercises 'What makes me happy?' and 'What am I not doing that I like to?', gardening was close to the top of my list. I began spending hour upon hour weeding and pruning, getting the garden back into order.

I also started to think about what you had said about giving and receiving. Suddenly it dawned on me that I was scared of loving. I decided to buy a dog. I've always loved animals and one of the losses when my wife and kids left was that they also took the family labrador. So I bought myself a pup. I've enjoyed her company. The responsibility of having to feed her prompted me to look after my own eating habits too.

It is remarkable how small things like seeing my roses bloom or playing with my puppy helped me to realise that all was not lost. One Saturday morning I woke up knowing I'd turned the corner. I wanted to communicate, to go out . . . to live.

I rang a couple of people who'd been at the seminar and arranged to meet them for a meal. I also phoned my mother who lives in the country and said I wanted to visit her. It suddenly hit me just how concerned she – and the rest of my family and friends – must have been. It struck me just how much worry I'd caused them by pushing them away. I'd been too caught up in my own self-pity to think of anyone else.

I now know that it is, as you say, up to me to choose to be happy!

Ken

Nothing magical happened at the seminar that Ken attended. What happened during that day was a break in the negative spiral that his life had become. He did this himself. The fact that he had mustered the energy – and courage – to attend the seminar, to do something about his life was, of itself, a positive turning point.

Coming out of isolation and being with other men and women who had gone through the ending of a relationship helped to put his break-up in perspective. The difficulties he'd encountered living singly were not unusual and were totally understandable. Focusing for a few hours on himself helped him to see things differently.

Change often takes time, patience and perseverance. It frequently helps to start with the simple and easily achieved.

If your committed relationship has recently ended you may find it difficult to know where to start. I suggest that you take things gently for a while. Grieving is a natural process. It often takes quite some time to work through. Even if your relationship was not a particularly happy one, it is likely that you will experience a sense of loss, anger, self-doubt and depression. Don't be surprised either if you feel resentment because a phase of your life has come to an end and you are embarking on the unknown which can be scary.

Some people jump straight into making a new life for

themselves, turning their backs on the hurt and distress of their past. They embrace change with gusto and look to the future with a surprisingly positive outlook. While there is nothing wrong with such an energetic approach to starting again, it can, however, be a way of avoiding the recognition and release of deeper feelings of pain and loss that are the residue of the ending of a relationship. If ignored these emotions are likely to simmer for a period of time in the subconscious and then to surface when least expected or desired. Grief that is not expressed is often the cause of seemingly inexplicable bouts of depression that may be experienced months or years after a relationship ends and which may jeopardise the potential of another developing.

## Widowed

If you are single again because of the death of a spouse it is important that your grieving does not prevent you from actively seeking to create a new life for yourself. You may feel your loss for a lifetime but if you let your grief and sadness prevent you from appreciating the opportunities that abound in life for happiness, you will waste much of the potential you have to give and to receive. You will also lose the chance to grow and thus risk leading a stunted existence till the day you also die.

Assuming responsibility for actively building a meaningful and happy life can be difficult at the best of times. For the widowed person it can be especially so if their life has been spent sharing most things with their partner. If you have lost your mate you have a tremendous challenge ahead – for you need to find a new formula for joy. As with all the other instances of living effectively as a single, I would suggest that a good starting point would be to take stock of yourself and your life to date. Reconsidering the exercises in the workbook could prove very helpful. Then open your eyes to the possibilities for developing companionship and pursuing interests that exist in your world right now.

A word of caution if you want to find someone else to share your life: many a widowed person has come to my consultancy wanting to find a partner to replace their

deceased mate. This is unrealistic and unfair, both to
yourself and any potential partner you may meet, as each
of us is unique. Be open to exploring and appreciating the
differences in each person you encounter. You may be
surprised to discover there are things you value in people
that you have never recognised before.

## Look before you leap again

One of the most potentially problem-fraught reactions we
can have to a relationship ending is impulsively to
rebound into another. Men especially seem prone to
jumping back into marriage or a partnership without taking the time to think about what they really want and need
in a relationship in the light of their past experience.

When I first spoke with him, David said he was anxious
to marry again despite the unhappy record he'd had to
date. While he realised that this might seem crazy, he
believed living without a partner was an empty and mean-
ingless experience.

After three trips to the altar, a bachelor's life seemed the
sensible option. Yet as a man in his forties with the prom-
ise of many years ahead, David thought that to resign
himself to a life alone would be a very heavy sentence, no
matter how sensible.

It became clear as we discussed his life experiences that
like so many men, David had never in fact lived alone for
more than a few months at any stage in his life. His is a
fairly typical story.

At 21 he left the security of his family home to marry
his childhood sweetheart. His young bride happily took
over looking after him where his mother had left off.

It was not until they had both turned 30 that David was
forced to face the fact that his marriage was on the rocks.
On the surface their relationship had seemed adequate
enough to David. He certainly was not on the look-out for
other women and he was putting so much energy into
climbing the executive ladder that he was relieved that Sue
did not seem overly interested in sex.

When Sue announced out of the blue that she had been
having an affair for over a year and was leaving him for
a man who 'really loved her', David was devastated. There

was nothing he could do or say. From his point of view he had been a good husband and provider. How could she be so wrong? Never again would he 'waste his life' with a woman who wasn't appreciative of what he had to offer!

However, the pattern was set to repeat itself. A few weeks after Sue and the children left, David covered his bruises with his best blue suit and went to a party. No sooner had he arrived at the gathering than a pretty dark-headed woman caught his eye. Except for the colour of her hair, she reminded him of Sue.

David could not believe his luck. Within a month April and he had decided to live together.

From the outset David had difficulty with April's sons. They resented him and there was tremendous tension.

For some years April and David managed to hold things together. Then, suddenly one day, April announced that she was going back to her former husband.

So David, now well into his thirties, found himself on his own again. Once more another 'ungrateful woman' had 'ruined his life'. He swore to himself that never again would he get involved with anyone with kids.

He decided he badly needed a break and a whole change in his life; he took a well-earned three month holiday and booked himself on a round-the-world cruise. He figured that this would be a way of having a total rest as he would not have to lift a finger to look after anything more than tending his wounds by enjoying the sun and relaxing.

Just two days out of port, David met Angela. When he first saw her, for a fleeting moment he thought that she could well be his daughter as she couldn't be much more than 18. He dismissed this thought when she showed obvious interest in him.

What a wonderful time those few months were. Hardly a moment were they apart and David had no need to dwell on the sadness he had left behind. Angela was a veritable angel whose smile magically healed his hurts.

As they made plans to be together and establish a home, David felt that this time everything would be fine. She would not leave him for a past love as she said that she had never had a serious relationship before. Nor did she have any children to cause him problems.

For a few years it seemed as if things were working.

Then things started to slide. Angela said she was bored. She did not have enough to occupy her. David was faced with a real dilemma: she said she wanted children. He felt, in turn, that now he was in his forties he was too old to handle an infant in his home. Besides, he had already experienced the negative effects children could have on a relationship and he'd just finished supporting his two from his first marriage.

So Angela decided to add interest to her life by taking up acting, something for which she had always thought she would have a flair. When Angela was offered a leading role in a film to be shot in Tahiti he dramatically asserted, after too many glasses of red one night, that it was Tahiti or their marriage. Next day he woke to discover that Angela had gone. Her note simply said 'There's more to my life than looking after you!'.

Since I first met David he has now been on his own for several months. He still hankers for someone to share with but he is starting to see that he can enjoy living on his own and that he can do many of the things he had depended on a partner to do for him. He is finding it interesting to explore who he is when he is on his own. He also realises that it is important that he stop and take time to think about what he might learn from the relationships he has had to date. He needs to see if there has been any pattern that he has been repeating that has led to the 'failure' of his three marriages.

When I last spoke to him, David told me that he could now see that he'd wanted a marriage like the one he believed his parents had had. He realised that he had assumed that all a happy marriage required was to find someone he cared for and who wanted to be with him. He'd expected that a wife would automatically create the happy home he'd had in his childhood as long as he pro- vided for her. He'd transferred the dependence he'd had upon his mother on to each of his wives without thinking of their needs beyond looking after, and sharing with, him.

Like many of us, David had believed that there was a set formula for a successful marriage. He had no idea about working on a relationship or considering the needs and expectations of a partner, or his own for that matter.

He has started to date women again but he now intends to learn from his experience and not jump into the first available partnership simply to avoid being alone. As he sees things now, he will make much more of a conscious effort to hear and understand what a woman's expectations are too. He now realises that it is vital to keep channels of communication clear and open and to accept that needs and wants are likely to change over time. Instead of being rigid in his attitudes he wants to be more prepared and be able to 'change gears' and keep a relationship alive. He believes he will have more to offer in a relationship next time, when he musters the courage to try again.

## Standing on your own two feet

Perhaps, like David, you are finding it difficult to be alone after a relationship has ended. It could be that you also have had little experience living on your own. The good news is that you do have a great deal to discover about yourself if you are prepared to do so. You may be surprised at how interesting a person you are. If, on the other hand, you find yourself to be dull and boring, being single again will help you to realise that it is up to you and not anyone else to take steps to develop yourself.

Maybe you also have been too dependent upon a partner for satisfying your needs and for giving your life purpose. Yet this is not being at the helm of your life, nor is it the foundation of mature and reciprocal love. Such dependency prevents you from being able to give and to receive love on the basis of free and conscious choice.

You do not have to be burdened with such dependency needs. You have the power to take charge of your life, to take up new interests, to initiate social activities, to develop friendships and to become more actively involved in the world around you. There is no need for you to be a limpet or boring. Become a mature and attractive companion, for yourself as well as for anyone else with whom you would like to share your leisure and, perhaps, your life.

Because they have traditionally been dependent upon men for their material well-being, to become single again can cause understandable feelings of helplessness in women, even in instances where a divorce settlement has left them financially well off. Especially for a woman who grew up before the influence of women's liberation, or who has never supported herself, the ending of a long-term marriage can demand a conscious effort to come to terms with the practical aspects of survival previously delegated to her mate. If she is to function effectively the woman who finds herself alone must learn to see herself and her abilities differently, to appreciate that she is potent, not powerless. To rush back into the arms of another man is not the answer and, for many women, suitable arms are not readily there.

I have met women who have no idea of how to write cheques and have only been inside a bank when accompanying their husband. In the 1980s this seems crazy yet it is true. There are women who do not understand the first thing about tax, paying bills, balancing their accounts, who have no idea of where or how their partners or husbands have organised their affairs.

The responsibility for managing the practical day-to-day affairs of life rests squarely on the shoulders of anyone who is single and though it can be difficult for the woman who finds herself suddenly single to accept and adjust to this fact, she must. The more a woman is able to provide for herself if need be, the less likely she is to be trapped in a relationship because she is dependent rather than because she chooses to be there.

## Challenge of the unknown

These days, more and more women are leaving marriages which but a decade ago would have held them for a lifetime, despite the unhappiness of their relationships. Until recently the vow 'for better or worse, for richer or poorer until death us do part' gave licence for couples to live in circumstances ranging from the sharing between soul-mates to a soul-destroying co-existence.

Jane is an example of a woman who decided to take the risk of leaving a long-term marriage.

When I first met her she was a youthful-looking woman in her late forties. Her vivacious personality and quick sense of humour were immediately apparent; assets that she believes had helped her tolerate the many unhappy years of her marriage.

Before her recent divorce, she had accepted that there was little in the way of caring or communication in her marriage. The first few years with Tim she sees as coloured by the romance of two 20-year-olds setting up independent house together. Yet as she looks back now, she believes that they had very few things in common even then, and that they very quickly grew apart. From her point of view, she changed and Tim did not in terms of interests, attitudes and approach to life.

For much of their time together Jane had felt that she was stagnating and these feelings of discontent caused her to feel a sense of guilt, to doubt her adequacy as a wife. For the last years of their marriage, they lived together but slept in separate bedrooms. She had gone against Tim's wishes and taken a part-time job. She still took care of the house and her family and spent her evenings with their teenage daughter. Occasionally she had a night out with some girlfriends she'd known all her married life.

Despite its limitations, Jane remained in the marriage, telling herself that this was important for her daughter. In reality she now sees that she feared taking the step into the unknown more than she disliked living in the empty security of the life she knew. Even though she enjoyed her job and knew that there were possibilities of her working full-time she also had doubts about how she could manage to support herself and her daughter if they left the family home.

Like so many women her age, Jane grew up in an era when divorce was virtually unheard of, when the criterion of a successful marriage was its longevity, when any married person worthy of the name would, without question, want to be able to say on their deathbed 'we made it, we lasted it to the end', even if not 'we were happy together'. Like countless other couples in sprawling middle-class suburbia, Jane and her husband lived separate lives behind the veneer of their red-brick home.

Jane now wonders why she had accepted for so long that she and her husband were 'sentenced' for life by a decision made before they were mature enough to know what this commitment meant. Yet her preparedness to live the lie of her marriage for so many years is not surprising. Only when she was confronted by Tim's dalliance did she feel she had the justification to leave.

Starting a new way of life can be frightening. Yet Jane found the reality not nearly as daunting as she had feared. She set up home with her daughter in a flat near the city and though she missed some of the comforts she had had while living with Tim, she was enjoying working full-time and no longer had fears about how she would survive in the economic sense.

In Jane's mind, the biggest issue she had to contend with in starting again was her relationships with men. However, while she expressed considerable trepidation about dating, she knew she did not want to live the rest of her life without a man.

It was understandable that after many years of marriage Jane was unsure about going out with men. Despite her growing confidence in her appearance and personality, she was anxious about handling sexual encounters. She also knew that there is a lot of competition for the available males among women in her age group. She was excited and hesitant but committed to her new adventure.

Starting again is rarely easy. Jane's situation was not nearly as negative as it can be for many men and women who experience the break-up of a marriage because she had maintained a relatively high level of self-esteem and kept her sense of humour, despite her past disappointments and her current doubts.

If you are single again, the path before you might be intimidating and uneven. However, if you approach the future positively and with the desire to surmount challenges, like Jane you will undoubtedly find rich rewards along your way.

# SINGLE AND AGED

*I*t is inevitable that in the later years of our lives the majority of us will experience being single. This is especially the case for women because they tend to live longer than men. Regardless of whether we live singly or in a partnership it is our responsibility to look to the future and consider how we might best make provision for the quality and security of our lives when we grow old.

At the practical level, it is important that we have adequate funds to look after ourselves, and accommodation that is well suited to our needs. To obtain the material security we require it is sensible for us to consider taking out appropriate insurance for the later years of our lives. This is especially the case for single people who cannot rely on the financial planning of a partner to provide for them. Your financial security is your own responsibility as a single person.

Suitable housing depends on our particular background, circumstances, needs and health. If fit and active we may choose to live alone in our own home or flat or have someone share it with us. Many people these days, be they single or coupled, are opting to move into a retirement village complex at an age where they can enjoy going out and about without worrying about domestic responsibilities. They also feel secure because professional nursing assistance is on call if needed.

Living with children or relatives can also be a very satisfactory way of being able to give and receive love and feel secure in old age – if this suits the temperaments and circumstances of all concerned.

As you will see in Part Four, some independent singles in their thirties are already thinking about how they might like to live several decades from now. At this stage it may be their preference to choose to live alone after retirement but they are planning to be in close proximity to people they care about. Friendship is very important to them now so it is not surprising they consider the best insurance policy for old age is to maintain and nourish these bonds.

Even if you are partnered do not shy away from discussing the matter of retirement, pensions, insurance and so on with your partner. Some people, especially women, when they find themselves suddenly alone, have no idea of how they will survive financially. If you are in a relationship or marriage it is vital that you ask directly and negotiate what provisions should be made. If past provisions are, in your opinion, inadequate, you must set in motion the necessary steps to correct the situation. It may be necessary for you to seek advice, either from a trusted member of your family, or better still, from your bank, family accountant or well-established investment and insurance broker. Matters such as death duties, pensions, superannuation and life insurance (both for yourself and your husband or partner) must be dealt with well in advance. The foundation, laid early, will ensure that your later years will be comfortable and lived in a manner of your choosing.

Younger people, even those who believe they may marry one day, should look carefully at the insurance options available. Begun early, these schemes often offer good cover for retirement at a very small initial investment. It is never money ill spent and, if in time your circumstances change, policies can often be merged or your affairs readjusted without great loss.

How would you like to spend the later years of your life? What can you do now to insure your future happiness?

I want to remind you that you need never be 'old'. Although the strength and capabilities of our bodies diminish during the later years of life, age is nevertheless a state of mind and our minds need stimulation if they are to thrive. Some people are old at 20, they fear meeting the challenges of life and deny their potential to develop. They have a set outlook on life and are unprepared to embrace change and to grow. Others, however, express their inner urge to expand their boundaries and are actively involved with life regardless of whether they are 20 or 90.

A few weeks ago I pushed a boundary for myself. I confronted my fear as I jumped from 2 000 metres on a tandem parachute. I was told I was rather courageous to do a first jump at the age of 37. I was surprised at this assumption. I couldn't help smiling when a few days later I learned that a month beforehand a woman well into her 60s had done the same thing.

I do not want to say that as you look to the possibility of being single in the later years of your life you should plan to jump out of planes. What I do want to point out is that if you look after your physical health and the material requirements you have to live satisfactorily then there is no reason why you shouldn't be able to look forward actively to exploring new possibilities and enjoying life until you die.

4

# Some singular lives

# SINGULAR EXAMPLES

*S*uccessfully *Single* is a combination of my own experiences, current research, and the experiences of others. I have known many people who live without partners; the task of writing this book made me look afresh at their lives. Among them are several who epitomise in some way what it means to be successfully single and I have chosen five particular individuals and interviewed them for this book.

Each one has, as do each of us, a story of his or her own; and every one is very different. While I do not suggest these examples as blueprints by which you should live your life, there is something to be learnt about some of the options available to you. And emerging clearly from them all is a sense of purpose, resolution and self-esteem.

# MARGO

*M*argo epitomises the successful single woman. Living singly has been a free choice. She has weighed up the alternatives: immensely attractive and in the prime of her life, she has had the option to marry and has determined to take a single path.

Y What does being single mean to you?

M The first word that comes to mind is freedom. It's being free to do what I want, when I want and how I want with whom I want. It's having choice. The picture that comes to my mind is sitting in my little apartment looking out at the trees, being alone and other people coming . . . lots of people . . . drinking too much, talking far too much, exploring ideas, not censoring what I am saying.

It's also being free to have different sorts of friendships. They're terribly important. I have so many different sorts of friendships and relationships that all need time . . . and I need time for myself, too. Being single therefore means having a lot of time to myself and for being very selfish. I don't make any apologies for that, I don't see that as pejorative at all but as a fact.

The thing is, I find myself very interesting. I really do need a lot of time.

Y When you think about your relationships, how does that highlight the advantages of being single for you?

M It means I can sleep all Sunday or whatever. As I freelance this doesn't matter. It means I can sleep through the day when I want to work through the night. It means, say, having muesli for dinner. It means not having to think about someone else . . . whether someone is going to be a little fragile if you haven't cooked a meal or if you don't want to sit down and have a drink with them or don't want to talk about what they want to talk about.

Y Do you think you always want to continue being in this single state?

M I think I do. But knowing how much I've changed in my lifetime – I've been through all sorts of phases which have been very, very significant and there's no way I'd ever take away from any phase because each has played an important part in my life – so I can really only talk now. I think that is another very liberating thing. When people talk about their feelings, about relationships and their ideas it's almost as though they're making a statement about what is to be 'forever' and I just don't see it that way. So all I can say now, at the moment, is that I love being single. I want to be single.

I can speak very definitely within a two year framework as I have very definite goals for the next two years. They revolve largely around my work which is at a very important and exciting phase and I need a lot of energy for it. There's no place in my life at the moment for a full-time or live-in lover or relationship. But I don't know that that is going to last forever. How could I know that? And the delightful thing that I see about life is nothing is forever.

Nothing is irreversible, aside from the biological dilemma that all we women know about and talk about until we are blue in the face, agonise about, cry about and laugh about. Aside from that, nothing is irreversible.

I may decide something different when I'm at the age of, say, 45. By then I imagine I'll be very successful. I will have achieved many of the goals that are so consuming now, particularly in my work. I can imagine in 10 years' time I might think 'Hmm, it's time for me to go to a Greek

island and write short stories'. I could meet anyone there,
as I could here in Sydney and say: 'Yes I'm relaxed and this
person understands my need for space' – if space is still so
important to me then. I might then well say to myself 'I
can live with him, I can even marry him if I want to'.

So when you look at 'what is', now, you can feel really
powerful about that but also feel really powerful about the
future . . . it doesn't stop tomorrow. What you set in train
now doesn't mean that it is forever. We can change, we
can alter our lives, if we just know that.

Y  I'm hearing someone who feels pretty powerful about the
direction of their life. Have you always felt like that?

M  No. And the time I felt least powerful and least certain
was the time when I was in my closest relationship. When
I say 'closest' I mean the physically closest relationship
which I have ever had which was living with someone . . .
that was the time I felt for the first time in my life
physically trapped. I remember sitting on the bed one day
after a terrible argument and just looking at the walls and
thinking 'I don't believe this'. I've read about women feeling trapped. Men don't feel trapped in the way that we do.
Because I'd given up the lease on my flat, I felt a really
tangible loss of flexibility and options. I remember saying
to my lover at the time – he was concerned as I was,
verging on hysteria – 'I feel trapped'. I looked at the door
and thought 'Where does that lead?' I didn't feel powerful.

When I finally mustered up the residue of any sem-
blance of power over my life and left, the only way I could
do it was to put myself on a plane and physically fly out
of that city to another one. One level of me saw the complete loss of power and the continuing loss of power and
on the same level was saying: 'Fuck it, do something. You
were good before. You moved yourself around the world.
You've been in relationships before this. You have had a
job in which you have performed well. You have moved
yourself from one city to another. Why is it that you feel
like crying all the time? That if this man were even to ring
up and say "Listen, come back" you might even do that.'
So there was that part of me looking at that.

And then at the other level, the part of me who was
being looked at was sitting there and thinking, 'I feel shit-
house. I don't think I'm ever going to get it together again.'

And in fact that took many years. The 'taking' I'm talking about was the getting back of confidence.

I used to look back to the years in my early twenties when I was a very confident person. Part of that confidence came from the arrogance of youth which I believe does exist. There was such a feeling of contrast. I couldn't help but say to myself: 'Whether it was arrogance of youth or not, I felt a bloody sight better than this then!'

Y   Did you feel as in control in your 'arrogant youth' phase because it seems to me it's the age when many people marry because they feel they should marry?

M   I felt absolutely in control. Mind you, looking at that age of 24, I'd come through university. I'd come through the Vietnam war era at university. I was at a radical university and we thought we had the world by the balls.

Y   You were a baby boomer?

M   I was a baby boomer. I was the eldest child with a wonderfully arrogant and ambitious father. I was destined to do what he did. He didn't want me to be the eldest son ever. He loved the fact that I was a girl. He didn't see a sexual difference in terms of achievement.

Y   You were very fortunate in that sense in not having the usual conditioning.

M   Yes. And he was also very influential in my feelings and my attitudes. He always sat at the head of the dining-room table. We all sat around and drank wine, we talked about things and my father over and over again said to all of us – there were three girls and a boy – 'You have choices, you can do anything you like, you can achieve anything that you want. It's to be achieved. Marriage is a wonderful thing but it's not it all.'

We have all taken that message and understood it and followed it. One of us has chosen to marry and has a beautiful relationship. The other three haven't chosen to marry but we've all had beautiful relationships and we are clear about our being single . . . and we've had to make decisions about that because the easiest decision it seems to me is to marry like everyone else. So to make a decision not to marry – and as a woman not to have children – requires considerable thought and working out.

Y   The choice not to have children: How have you processed that because it is a big decision for a woman to make?

**M** It's been something I've thought about ever since I first slept with a man at the age of 18. Then it used to occupy most of my waking hours as I was having a sexual relationship with this man while I was at university and of course I wasn't taking any contraceptive measures. And while I was still intellectually liberal, in those days it was very difficult to go to a doctor and get a contraceptive pill, particularly in the city I was living in which was a small city. We had family doctors and there weren't family planning clinics – or any that I knew about.

So I certainly thought about babies all the time, mainly in terror that there might be one growing inside me. I progressed from that stage and moved out of that relationship and then flung myself wholeheartedly into the free-loving of the seventies. Thank God I was around in those years. Now it is not so easy.

At that time I was able to get the pill so the problem of becoming pregnant wasn't the same consideration it had been before. The issue became: 'Shall I have a baby or not?' I didn't really give much thought about this then for four or five years. It certainly wasn't an issue. I wasn't planning on getting married.

I was living in another city by now, a very exciting city. I was working and being with people who were politically aware, who were very intellectually aware . . . though perhaps not so much emotionally aware. Certainly we felt very powerful about the world and thought that the world was to be experienced and experimented with. At that time the women's liberation movement was very much present. Women were out with spray cans painting fences. Newspaper articles were about inconsequential things like bra burning but certainly we were made aware of the movement. It was happening. Among the topical issues was 'Do women have to have babies?'.

After four years of not thinking about it very much at all I started to think about it again. I had a few lovers, one in particular I was very drawn to. I had very desultory conversations with him as a foray into the idea of having a baby. I was certainly not interested in marrying. It was more of a romantic notion, the romantic possibility of having a child . . . not terribly practical and it didn't last very long.

I kept changing my mind about it until I was thirty when I decided no, absolutely no . . . and it wasn't a result of saying to myself 'Well, I'm turning 30, hadn't I better make the decision about this?' In fact in my thirtieth year there was the possibility that I and a lover were going to spend the rest of our lives together. We spent time talking about it and one of the issues that came up was 'will we have children?'. I remember saying 'NO'.

I didn't want children, while he did. He already had children of his own. I believed at the time – and I still believe now – that his desire for kids was very much as an expression of our relationship and it was very important on that level. So for me to hang out and say 'no' . . . and remember I loved this man very much . . . makes it possible for me to look back at that time and say: 'Yes, that really was the time when I was very clear that I did not want children.'

It was also the year that my only sister who is married had her first child. I remember when her daughter was born thinking that it was the most wonderful thing to have happened, yet at the same time saying to myself, 'she is not mine', and feeling very glad about that. Since then I've become an aunt a number of times. I have some very strong ideas about the role of an aunt . . . it is a very magical thing . . . an indulgent thing as well. You're free to be wonderful to the children without having to do the unpopular and complex things like disciplining, chastising . . . I haven't ever considered having children since then. I certainly don't see biologically that I have much time. That doesn't worry me. Those years are going to pass very quickly. It's not going to happen. I love children very much and I think I am a wonderful aunt. I write stories for the children and fortunately my nieces' and nephews' parents see myself and my unmarried and 'unchilded sister' as very central in their children's lives, now and in the future. We often talk about the place we will have for them later on. They see us as being able to teach their children things they won't be able to teach so well.

Y How, as a single person, do you have many of your needs met and what gives meaning in your life? You have touched on how your maternal needs are being met. What about other needs?

**M**  I'm very clear about my needs. My needs are very strong. I'm excessive in every way. I have very strong emotional needs, I have very strong sexual needs, I have very strong intellectual needs, and I have very strong nonsensical needs.

What do I consider I require to meet my emotional needs? Having people available around, having people loving me on all sorts of levels, every level. Having people who understand me, having people who will put up with all my irrationality, who will not question when I want them, why I want them or what I want them for. Friends who make me feel wonderful. When I have a new dress, I walk in and they say 'you look wonderful'. When I write a story they know what I want to know . . . I don't want to know the whole truth!

**Y**  Do you feel loved?

**M**  Oh yes!!

**Y**  Why are you loved?

**M**  I'm loved because I love, because I have a lot of energy. I have a lot of friends and it's because I have a lot of interests, a lot of ideas about things, I laugh a lot, I'm stupid, I cry. It's because I'm excessive I think that people love me and because I'm not afraid to show things. I can be really nasty as well, really horrible and short tempered but at least people know. I don't pretend things.

So my emotional needs are met by many, many people. I have a lot of acquaintances but I also have a lot of close, close friends. We're now talking about my being 36, I'm not 18 or 24. I don't count my close friends on one hand. I count my close friends on both hands and on the toes of both feet as well . . . and probably more. Over these years I still have as my closest friends some people I've known since I was at school.

As I have gone on through life I have met many people. I have many friends. I mean this sincerely. I don't have two friends I tell everything to – I probably have 25! It sounds implausible but it's true. So my emotional needs are met through these people. Now these people are old school friends, old university friends, they are old work friends, they are women primarily, they are ex-lovers, they are my family, they are my gay friends . . . I'm categorising but I can very easily. They are also new friends, people I meet who have something in common, where we have a meeting point.

I want to talk about my female friends. They are terribly, terribly important in my life. I can speak to my female friends about the things that really matter more than I can speak with men. And having had many lovers, and many platonic male friends, and many homosexual male friends, and many close male friends I can confidently say that it's the women who meet my emotional needs.

It is also the women who stimulate me intellectually, who meet my intellectual needs. It's the women who listen, who articulate well, who don't get scared witless in some of the areas we go into, who don't use emotional blackmail or bargaining. So I have to say that I delight in the number of female friends I have and they are women who are doing the most interesting things. They're the ones who are taking the risks.

Y   Interestingly enough, in terms of what I'm hearing you say about how much you really connect with women, your sexual choice is men.

M   Oh yes, I love men. When I say I love them, I can't resist them. I've also been lucky in that respect. When I say 'lucky' lots of people wouldn't think I'm lucky because what they would see is an attractive, very bubbly, fairly rounded, sexually appealing woman who has, on the face of it, no man. I live with no man. To the public at large I have no boyfriend and I'm certainly not married and I have no kids. And so to people who really set marriage or a constant relationship as a criterion for success and happiness, well then, I wouldn't meet that. It is, of course, total and utter nonsense.

What heterosexual males have for me is sexual attraction. Most of my significant encounters with heterosexual males have been primarily on a sexual basis. Though I would prefer it, it just seems to be very difficult to find the levels of emotional and intellectual interest I want.

I've got to make that really clear. I don't mean that every available – or unavailable, as it doesn't matter much to me which – heterosexual male I meet I have sex with. Most heterosexual men have no attraction for me. I must explain something else about that. The three lovers of my life who are current lovers – and have been from 10 to 17 years off and on but who have endured – I met within six years of each other. Since then I haven't met many men who have interested me on all levels – sexually, intellectually, and emotionally.

**Y** So is one of the reasons that you are happily single because there is a paucity of available interesting men for you?

**M** Yes. Yes. Absolutely yes.

**Y** That seems a reality for a lot of women.

**M** It's pretty hard going with men sometimes . . . they don't think the same.

**Y** What's the down side for you about being single?

**M** Something I'd like to talk about first is something that is no longer a 'down side' for me but has been in the past. As I've said earlier, men find me attractive. However I don't conform to your Vogue notion of attractiveness. I am two stone overweight – I'm a very large woman. I certainly don't fit conventional notions of attractiveness. And there have been times in my life when I've really worried about it and gone on terribly strict diets. I used to lose three stone at a time. In fact I am sure I could measure my weight loss and my weight gain over the past 10 years in tons – cumulatively speaking! I don't diet any more.

**Y** You were trying to conform to the stereotyped image of what you should be as an attractive woman?

**M** Yes, yes. I now look at photos of myself at the skinniest times. I used to have three sizes – small, medium and large – and I had three wardrobes as well. I tossed them out earlier this year. I just have the large one now. When I was slim I often felt fat. I was in such agony for no reason at all. Can I say that there was not much difference anyway? Regardless of my weight, the world didn't cave in, nor was there a posse of men beating their way to my door. There was no difference that I can detect from now when I'm large, and comfortable and going well.

In fact I think in terms of being attractive to the opposite sex I would say that I am more attractive now at the age of 36 than ever before yet I'm heavier than I've probably ever been and certainly more wrinkled. I'm sure that's so.

**Y**  Why is that?

**M**  I'm more relaxed.

**Y**  More confident with yourself?

**M**  Yes. These days how I look, how I behave, how I want things are according to my standards. They are not set by anyone else. Maybe my standards are pretty crazy. They certainly don't conform to the ones I judged myself by previously that seemed to conform to the consensus of how things should be.

**Y**  Yet, nevertheless, I hear that there are some negatives for you being single. What are they?

**M**  I imagine that they are the reverse side of the coin for married people. Everybody has down sides. There are certainly down sides living my life the way I do. As I've mentioned before, I have three lovers. For many reasons, one of which is primarily distance, I don't see them as often as I'd like. Certainly not as much as one would in a married relationship, a live-in relationship or a committed full-time partnership.

The main down side is that we get out of synch. When I want to see one of them, often it is not possible. That's frustrating and sometimes agonising as the whole relationship gets called into question. It is not only that they're not available. It's often me who is not available. As I mentioned earlier I have a very busy job. I'm freelancing and so much energy has to go into that. I've also mentioned all the other people who are in my life. They also take precedence sometimes. So we're out of synch in that sometimes I want one of them and they're not available and at other times I'm not available to them.

**Y**  What about loneliness versus aloneness? Do you know about loneliness?

**M**  No, not really. I know about being lonely occasionally, for a few hours or a day. Especially when one of my lovers, the person I want to be with, is not available. But I don't know about existential loneliness. I do not have a feeling of being lonely. I often feel alone because it's factual. But I like being alone so it's not a problem. Most of the time I'm alone it is through choice.

**Y**  You've set up so many alternative options. I guess you needn't ever have to be alone.

M   But I want to be alone – quite a lot really – to read, think, write, listen to music, stare out the window. That's a point I want to make. My lovers, though very central, are not the centre of my life. Though that's not always been the case. When my first love affair ended I felt terrible and lost.

Y   What gives a sense of meaning to your life, what motivation?

M   For me it is very much a sense of self. It is a sense of my own place in the world as distinct from anyone else. I don't see myself as 'half of a relationship', whatever relationship that might be. I don't see myself primarily as 'a daughter', 'a lover', 'a sister', 'a wife'. I see myself as ME.

Y   How do you get over the problem of being a small cog in a big wheel? If we look at the world today, we're pretty small and finite.

M   In the overall scheme of things I'm not large and that doesn't worry me. I don't play on a world stage. I do inasmuch as I think about the world and I feel frustrated and hopeless about some of the world problems. How I handle that is to bring it back to the practical level and say 'OK I live here. I do this. I have these goals. I think these things. These people are in my life'. And on that stage I make things happen. I affect things and that gives my life a sense of potency and meaning.

# BRENDA

*B*renda is divorced and a mother with two children. She is single by choice but clear-eyed about the responsibilities and realities of single parenthood.

Y   What is being single for you?

B   Being single for me is having total responsibility for my two children, of being responsible for all actions and decisions and not having to refer to anybody else for any kind of advice.

Y   Are you enjoying that?

B   Oh yes. And being financially independent, although I must admit I worked throughout my married life as well, but at that stage I used to give whatever money I earned to my husband. Now whatever I earn is mine and I don't have to ask permission to have anything.

Y   Do you see that sort of independence as being a big advantage of being single?

B   I think that being financially independent is a big thing. From what I gather in so many instances money is always such a bone of contention. I'm quite an extravagant person and that was always a terrible issue in my marriage.

**Y**  What have been the disadvantages for you?

**B**  The children found it very difficult to adjust. They resented the fact that I was the one that dissolved the marriage, particularly my daughter who is now 11.

**Y**  What was the core of your dissatisfaction?

**B**  It's so difficult. It's so many things. First of all our sexual relationship was nil. Secondly, I don't think I'm cleverer or more intelligent but perhaps my interests developed and we grew in different directions. There was no mental stimulation whatsoever. There was never a fight or argument – never any kind of discussion. Life was so monotonous – there were no ups or downs. I felt that life offered more to me than just that. He did not make any decisions. Everything was left to me and I got to the stage where I felt he was a third child, and more of a responsibility than the children were. I think that's when I realised that things were just not right and it was up to me to make the change if I wanted to.

**Y**  You present as a very sexual woman. How did you manage not having a sexual relationship?

**B**  I felt that this was my lot in life, and I had chosen it and therefore I had to put up with it. And it's funny, for the first 11 years I never had an affair, I never looked at anybody else. I did nothing until I realised the marriage was at its end.

**Y**  How did you cope?

**B**  Well I was always so busy. I worked. School started at 7.50 and I left the house at 7.30. And I would often go to bed at 8.00 at night – I was exhausted.

**Y**  So you didn't have time to think about the problems?

**B**  Right. They never ever presented themselves. That was my life – that was the way I had chosen to live. I entertained an enormous amount. I was forever having dinner parties and there were always people around. We had a lovely house with a beautiful big swimming pool and Sundays were open house. Ted virtually never came outside. He didn't like being in the sun. And I was quite happy. I had people around me and that was that.

**Y**  So people are important to you?

**B**  Yes. Well I had to find stimulation somewhere, and that was another thing, Ted never had friends of his own. All his friends were basically my friends – friends that I had made.

Y   What really prompted the choice to leave? Obviously you
    had a choice?
B   Because life was just so intolerable with him.
Y   So you didn't need to grieve when you left?
B   No, the marriage was so dead. I must admit that once I
    was on my own I didn't really go out much at first. There
    was a man I was having an affair with but he lived inter-
    state so I didn't see him that frequently. But after a few
    months I was ready to face the world, to go out and meet
    people and to live a proper life. Up until then I wasn't. I
    was just trying to find my feet, to see where I was going
    and what I wanted and to establish myself as a single
    person with responsibility to the children.
Y   Was that hard?
B   Not really. There was such a burden lifted from my
    shoulders. My flat became my haven. I think it has a very
    warm friendly atmosphere. People come in and say this.
    When I was married, particularly the last few months, I
    used to almost feel a blind coming down on me as I drove
    into the driveway and I used to think I was driving into
    jail, driving into prison. It had just such an awful atmos-
    phere about it. There was such tension.
Y   Would you ever have another relationship that was one-
    to-one and with commitment?
B   Oh I would, but it would be with a totally different kind
    of person. I would choose a far stronger personality and
    someone that I regard as a success. I regarded my husband
    as a failure and I don't think I could live with a man who
    I didn't respect and who I didn't feel was a success in his
    own right.
Y   So you've learnt from this first marriage of yours what you
    now would like to have in a relationship?
B   Oh yes, oh yes. I think respect and trust are two of the
    most important things one needs to have and they are
    things which are either there or they are not there. If it's
    broken I don't think you can rebuild that respect and
    trust.
Y   How would you feel if you were to see that the rest of your
    life would be lived as a single person?
B   I wouldn't really mind, so long as there are people around
    me and that I'm out and about.
Y   So you're not desperate to get married again?
B   Oh no, no. My children really want me to remarry and

they get very upset when I talk about plans in the long term on my own. My son particularly will say, 'But Mum, aren't you going to get married again?' And I say: 'Well, if the opportunity arises and I feel the time is right, possibly I might; but I might not.' People seem to think it won't be long and I'll be in marriage number two, but I will think very seriously before I ever commit myself again.

Y   Why do you think the kids would like you to marry again?

B   I think for the security of the home unit, having a man in the family and being a conventional family unit.

Y   How do they react to you going out with other men?

B   That's a big bone of contention. Al, the fellow that I had interstate, stayed with us a lot when we first moved to the flat. The children became very close to him and really adored him in a way. When I decided to start going out with other men (he is a very traditional sort of person) he said he could not tolerate the thought of my going out with someone else.

   He was insanely jealous. It was all or nothing, so that he expected me to behave like a married woman while he was galavanting around Australia while still married to his wife. He could not see that as any kind of issue. Obviously I didn't love him enough because otherwise I would be quite happy with the status quo. The children were very upset, particularly my son. He was absolutely distraught and his words were 'you're married to Daddy and you left him. Then you were in a relationship with Al and you have left him too' – almost as if to say will you ever have any kind of permanent relationship with a man again.

Y   Something very interesting in talking with you is that you are able to speak as a single mother of the disadvantages and problems of being a single parent. And one of them I'm hearing is that the children want you to be in a permanent relationship, and that must be difficult.

B   My daughter resents me going out with other men. She wants me to give her my undivided attention. My son now accepts that I go out with other people. I think my daughter would prefer me to have a steady relationship rather than go out with different men.

Y   Do you tell the kids that you're going out with someone different, or do you keep it to yourself?

B   No, I do tell them. Whoever it is normally comes to fetch me so the children always meet the man I'm going out with, unless it's a weekend when I'm on my own at the flat and they don't see him. If they are home I always introduce them and they will sit and chat.

Y   Do you think that could be more unsettling than helpful?

B   Well you know it's so difficult to know what is the correct thing to do, because when I discussed this with a therapist she said 'You have a life to lead, and particularly under the circumstances your daughter must know that she cannot dominate your life and that you have got to have time on your own and that there will be times when you are with other people.'

Y   How do the men react?

B   None have reacted adversely at this point in time. One man in particular that I met about six months ago who has been single all his life was totally unused to going out with women with children. When he came you could almost feel the animosity in a way, and the children did not like him much. I see him quite regularly, not every week but every couple of weeks, and gradually things have sorted themselves out and last week he said how terrific the children were.

Y   Do you see it as a potentially serious relationship?

B   No, he will never get involved with anyone. He is single forever.

Y   How do you manage your sexual life with the children? Is that an issue?

B   Well, I think it could be. I don't like having sex with somebody in my flat when the children are there if it's not a permanent relationship. If it's a permanent thing then fair enough. At the moment they think that I don't sleep with anyone and there's nothing discussed. I feel that that is something that is very much my private life and I don't at this particular point discuss it with them. It's never been an issue, it's never come up as such.

Y   Is it part and parcel of the whole thing that there will be a number of broken hearts along the way?

B   Yes. I've experienced a really broken heart – I was shattered I must admit. But, you bounce up again and you see what life will bring now.

Y   You sound very positive and very optimistic.

**B**  Well I have to be. For a couple of weeks I was very upset and very miserable, distraught, and I think perhaps I grieved then the grief I should have grieved at the end of my marriage. It was that type of mourning almost.

**Y**  How do you see your life now?

**B**  Now is a period of change. I've been teaching for 15 years and have decided that that chapter is going to close. I will definitely change my profession and enter the world of commerce because I feel that's the next step; that's my progression. I've been in a protected work environment all my life and I'm now ready to tackle the wide open world.

**Y**  It sounds very exciting. Do you think the ending of the marriage has been part of a . . .

**B**  I think I have boundless energy and I think it has been the catalyst in my life. And I then became introspective and decided what I wanted out of life, what I would do with the rest of my life; which way I wanted to go and how to go about it.

**Y**  Have you always had such a strong sense of your own power to do what you want?

**B**  Perhaps I had power but I had a very dominating father, a very strong aggressive man who put me down always. Now everybody says I'm so confident, but I lacked confidence completely while I was unmarried under my parents' roof. Even at uni I had virtually no confidence. 'Shut up you don't know anything', that was my father's response. Children were seen and never heard. Even as a teenager I had absolutely no confidence because Dad sapped it all. And perhaps the one good thing out of the marriage was that my confidence grew, and I did things and I experimented with things which came off and therefore I became more and more confident. Possibly I then realised that what I thought and what I did was not so stupid and was not so idiotic, and I could do things on my own without having to lean on A, B or C.

**Y**  Tell me, in terms of anyone reading the book and thinking about their lives and their options, especially someone with children, what sort of tips would you like to give; what are the sorts of things you would like to say that would be helpful?

**B**  First of all not to be frightened of what you think is right. If you feel that you want to make a move and go out on your own or do certain things – do it. Don't be frightened by what Joe Bloggs would say or what the neighbour or aunt would say. If you feel it's right for you – do it. You are responsible for who you are and what you are, and if you don't make the conscious decision to make a move or to make a change you will just carry on with the same sort of problem. The children will follow. I think they will gain from you being more confident, from you being happy, because being in an unhappy, unsatisfying relationship must rub off onto the children. They must feel some sort of sadness, tension, unhappiness, even if it's subconsciously there.

Y  Do you think there's the argument that you are being very selfish in making these sorts of decisions?

B  A lot of people do say that, but to me to sacrifice your entire life for the children means you're not giving them anything better because you are living as an unfulfilled person and therefore if you are unfulfilled you behave in a way that is not positive or behave like a martyr.

Y  Similarly, you should not only be a mother but also be a woman who has relationships and her own life?

B  Absolutely. I don't feel that a mother must martyr herself. My mother said to me 'I gave my life up for you children.' I don't think any mother has to do that – they must share it with them but they have their own life to lead. Children must realise that there are certain times and places that are for adults alone and not for them.

Y  Do you have a strong network of friendships? Is this something that's important to you?

B  Yes, I have two very close friends – couples, and it's quite interesting that I'm equally friendly with the husbands and the wives. It's not just the wife that's my friend. So they are four close friends. And then of course I have a wide circle of friends and acquaintants, but these four are the ones I can ring at any time of the day or night and they are I suppose my surrogate family.

Y  Have they helped make it possible for you to be happy as a single?

B  Yes, both couples have included me often when going out and by just being there. In no way at all have they put any slant on me being single as being wrong – it's made no difference to the relationship.

Y  Would your family like you to remarry?
B  Yes. I come from a very traditional family. Everyone went
   to school; university was an absolutely automatic progression – there was never any discussion about not going
   on. Once you got your degree you worked a little bit, got
   married, had children and settled down. That was the
   progression. Both my parents were professional people.
   My mother never worked – was always at home with the
   children. To them that is the ideal – being married and
   living as a family unit. At the moment it's always 'Poor B.
   I wonder how she's coping!' And I keep saying I'm as
   happy as the day is long.

# PETER

*P*eter planned for five years to leave his marriage because of the strong philosophy he has about personal growth and individuality.

Y   What does being single mean to you?

P   Freedom, a feeling of identity, individuality – that's part of it. Loneliness is there – it's an aloneness mainly, but there is a time when you do feel lonely. But it also creates that space that you create for yourself. For me, it's meant that I've been able to process so many things so quickly and there's been, I believe, a lot of personal growth operating. It's been far faster than anything I've ever experienced before. It's opened up my potential to be the sort of person I want to be and it's allowed me to take risks I couldn't take before. Despite the fact there have been times that have been sad and lonely (and I've seen my actions in moving out of a long-term relationship as being quite traumatic for my ex-wife) I've never ever doubted that my action is right. So at this point in my life I see myself as having set the scene for moving through the rest of my life the way I want to.

Y  What's the scenario for the rest of your life?

P  I've got pretty good ideas about the short term and the long term. I'm very aware that the people I want to have around me are energy givers rather than energy takers. I want to associate with people who enjoy the energy I give and enjoy my positive approach to life, enjoy my need to take risks and to reach out and keep expanding. I'm a little tired of being around people who keep setting parameters to the way they want me to live so that they feel comfortable with it. Unfortunately I'm talking about the majority of society and probably almost 90 per cent of my previous peer group. I posed a threat to them because I didn't conform to the safe way they wanted to live their lives. They felt insecure and they judged and I felt very judged.

   In terms of relationships I've got to the point after a fair amount of experimentation and a fair amount of frenzied activity where I would like to have a relationship which I see as a primary relationship which is contracted on a year or two years, or maybe on a longer basis as time goes on, but being very clear in terms of the fact that it has an end and then would be renegotiated. The contract would mean that there would be sexual fidelity exercised but there would be, beyond that, total freedom for both parties to pursue relationships, activities. I would see it as being a very successful relationship, with each partner actively supporting the other to follow those things they are really wanting to do. In other words to help the other person in the relationship to achieve at the highest level in terms of their life while they do the same for you.

Y  Is that what you see growth to be?

P  Exactly, I think that's what it's all about. Most of all I like seeing people being happy and also trying new things, experimenting, reaching out, and I'll do everything I can financially, spiritually or whatever to help people I care about to reach levels of achievement that are important for them.

   What you find in life is that once you start reaching out and taking risks you're immediately branded as being selfish, because really you should be living the sort of life that other people want you to live so that they feel safe. I became very aware of the fact that you should never ask other people what they think would be right for yourself because, with the best will in the world, most people will always tell you what is right for them, even though they think they're telling you what they think is right for you. My goal I guess is to expand at a rate where I'm reaching out and doing new things. I'm learning another language at the moment and to me that's breaking new ground. It's something I've wanted to do for a long time. I want to begin writing and I have a very clear idea of how that will be when I do it. Even ten years into the future, I have a very clear vision of myself living in Europe for a part of my life. They're all things on the drawing board and I'm working towards them.

Y   So change is comfortable for you?

P   Yes. My greatest criticism of people is their fear of change.

Y   How did you handle a 22-year-old marriage and what really brought that to an end?

P   It held together for most of that time through our sheer compatibility, good sense, respect and love for each other. But there was no intimacy. My wife and I achieved a lot of things as two people. We're administratively very good, our kids got on well with us and vice-versa. The first year I was married I started studying and that continued for another 11 years. I've always had a project going which diverted me, so I never put everything into the relationship. It just worked well. It was cohabitation, a very good support system for the kids but there was never anything else there.

Y   And yet a lot of people, would say, 'what else do you want? It sounds like you had a lot going for you.'

P   Yes, we did. In fact many people set us up as a model, and when I explained to them that I was leaving they were incredulous.

But my observation has been that people, especially when they've been in a relationship for a long time, in most cases teeter on the edge of getting out of the relationship – they look towards the future and what they could achieve – but it's the habit and the fear that drags them back and they collapse back into the relationship. Maybe it's a comfortable thing but they live on to the end of their lives supporting each other financially because economically it's viable to do so. As they get older they can slip each other pills. To me that's too high a price if all you're going to do is be around so you're not on your own. I would rather die on my own and have experienced life at the highest level.

To me you've got to continue risking. You don't get to a point where you say I'm 45 or whatever and soon I'm going to be 50 – now's the time I really need to start thinking about the future and security. This relationship's been here for 20 years, I know it's not everything I want, but it's secure and safe. To me that's a bloody bore – an absolute bore.

Y   Can you envisage remaining single for the rest of your life?

P   I'll certainly never remarry in the sense that it's understood in our society. I would certainly like to think that I'll be involved in one or perhaps more relationships in which I experience the ultimate in terms of intimacy and caring and love for another person. Also, at the same time being given total freedom to experience the life I want. Apart from the issue of sexuality which I mentioned earlier.

Y   Why can't a primary relationship work without open sexuality for you?

P   Well, I think there was a time when it could, and I see this as a matter of progression. In fact, if you had asked me that question 12 months ago I would have guaranteed you that I could have a perfectly good relationship and still have the freedom to experience my sexuality with a number of other relationships and feel quite OK about it. I don't know whether it's just a condition of becoming older. I suspect it's an outbreak of the processing I've done in the last eight months since I've been living on my own.

I've reached a point of saying, OK I can keep trying to find something new which is exciting sexually, but I find that there's so much bloody repetition now that I suspect that they're few and far between. There's occasionally some lady who's very in touch with herself in terms of her sexuality and who's a lot of fun and very exciting to be with – but they are very, very few and far between. They're usually older women too, who've spent a lot of years getting to that point.

Y   Are you clear about your expectations in that sexual situation? Do you make it clear to the woman?

P   That's an interesting one, because I've always been very clear, with the exception of two relationships. All of the others I've made very clear that all I offer is that I care for them while we are together and also have affection for them as friends, but no ongoing obligation whatsoever. And I clearly tell them that there are other people with whom I have that sort of involvement.

Y   Are they usually a one-night-stand situation?

P   No, never. I mean there have been times when I've met people and there's been a lot of physical chemistry operating and maybe on the second or third meeting there might have been a sexual encounter, but in the main they have been people I've known for quite some time. Funnily enough some of them are people I've known for many years who I'd met when they were married or I was married, and there's been an interest there. Now because I'm free and maybe they're free or whatever, there have been additional dinners, etc, and it's moved towards this. But I'm fairly circumspect and am not into one-night stands. I think there are a lot of health hazards involved and also I don't feel all that good operating in that sort of way.

Yet, while I was very clear, I wasn't always clear enough unfortunately. Some of those encounters have meant that I've got friendships that are really important to me and which are now non-sexual, they unfortunately are in the minority. In most cases the 'you owe me' element is introduced, and the moment that happens I withdraw completely. The level of intimacy was always fairly low anyway because I don't believe you can operate at an intimate level when you're saying in the same breath, listen I don't want to be involved. There was a very high recreational ingredient in it, and I think that began to teach me that I was hurting people.

When it stopped being important for me to have to prove to myself that I could keep attracting someone when I needed to, I felt that I was growing, and I felt: 'Why put people through that?' So the next stage was: OK what do you really want?

I want excellence in a relationship. I don't want it to be guaranteed forever but I want to be physically attracted and the woman would probably need to be fairly attractive because there's no doubt that the physical attractiveness of a woman is very important to me. The other ingredient that is so important is self-awareness. I really couldn't be involved with a woman who was not aware of what was going on within herself.

Y  How do you handle accusations like 'you're selfish'?

P  I used to defend myself against them. I think I probably am in the terms a lot of people see life. But I also realise if I'm going to be happy and fulfilled and die knowing I've squeezed every ounce of potential out of myself, then I have to take responsibility for my own life. I'm not prepared to sit back and say well I'm not going to do that because all these people depend on me.

I have some conflict with my ex-wife because when I have the kids they have to fit in with the things I'm doing. My ex-wife finds it very difficult because she sees her role in life as always being there for the children. That's an avoidance because you can always hide behind the children and say I don't have to grow, I don't have to experience. How can I? When the children grow up I will start. It doesn't work that way. I'm sometimes even accused of being selfish by my children, but it doesn't hurt any longer. I almost feel that I wear it like a badge.

Y  Did you try to improve the actual communication with your wife?

P  No, I don't think I did. It's almost as though I didn't want to, and yet I'm aware of having a very deep level of care and affection for her, and I think probably love. If anything was to happen to her it would really deeply affect me because I care for her very much as a person, but I just don't have in me the resources to be the traditional husband she wants.

Y  Was your wife wanting something else of the marriage?

P  She wanted a traditional marriage. She wanted to be able to plan our future and retirement together, and see the future clearly. I just found that so claustrophobic. So I don't think I put much into the marriage. I think I put more into my secondary relationship where I was very deeply in love with this person and I set a program then that I would be out of my marriage in five years, which is what I did. I wouldn't do it the same way again. It was incredibly painful. It's far better to do it quickly and let the grief work intensely, but fast. I had done most of my grieving by the time the end came. There's a bit of residual stuff from time to time. Yet it was easier for me. I picked

SOME SINGULAR LIVES 171

the time and place when I left although I had said all along when it was going to be.

Y  So what would you say to a man who's separating at the moment?

P  If you can, be prepared to be lonely and don't run from it. It's so easy to do. On an evening when you are sitting on your own and you start to feel alone, the compulsion to snatch the phone and ring a friend or ring a lady and make a date, whatever, just to make contact, is very strong. If you can sit and observe what's going on for you – ie I am feeling this way but I didn't need that; I'm OK on my own; I need people sometimes but I don't need them all the time; and I can cook well enough at the moment.

When I first moved out on my own I didn't look after myself particularly well. Now I really take pride in the sort of food I cook for myself. I take pride in the way my flat looks. They are all very important extensions of myself, and people who walk in who knew me in my old flat say it's totally different this way. The statement is there that this is mine – don't try and change it – because this is me. It's not half of somebody else. It's me. And I'm important. I'm very important as a potential friend, lover or whatever – don't take me cheaply. I value myself and I set a very high standard on a relationship, friendship, or whatever.

There will be that early stage of doubt when you want to jump into another relationship because someone is saying you matter. You frantically run around telling yourself that you are important because all these people want you, but then if you can slow down and work through a few of those nights when it is a bit lonely and get in touch with your feelings, you will stop fearing being on your own. In fact those times will become really important to you. And that's when the growth happens and that's when the processing accelerates, and that's when the answers start emerging.

You're confronted every day with statements in the press about how right it is to be married and that the nuclear family is really the answer, and it's just the poor state of civilisation at the moment which is not allowing it to work. I believe that you've got to be very aware of the fact that you can be brainwashed by well-meaning friends who are still married, sometimes in absolutely abysmal relationships. But because society deems them to be OK – the fact that you're still connected to another person for x number of years – makes them OK. The quality is so often questionable.

I have experienced the fact that anybody who makes the choice of being single is going to come under a lot of attack in the most subtle ways.

Y   What about the person who is single not because they have chosen it but because of the circumstance – they see it as circumstance – their partner has left them, or they haven't met someone they want to be with?

P   I think there can be nothing more devastating than to be left and not to see clearly that there are other people around who can fill the gap in a relationship. But there are tremendous advantages to a single relationship, and to a single way of life. If there are children there are certainly pressures in being a single parent, but they also can be really interesting, because a lot of quality can be derived from being a single parent – the time you have with your kids is quality time, and if you communicate at a pretty good level with your ex-partner the kids can be winners.

But the single person who is lonely and has not got a relationship on the horizon to look to, should look at some of the advantages: their ability to make choices, limitless choices of where they are going with their life; whether they want to travel; the sort of job they want. If they were in relationships they wouldn't have these choices.

Once the grieving goes and the self-esteem begins to grow (and that needs input and probably some sort of support group to bring it about) they will meet people in similar situations and an excitement begins to mount and they will say 'There are all these possibilities and I'm not stopped, I'm free to do it, and I've got all that experience of having this relationship behind me.' And if it's been a long one and you're really fair, you realise so many things you've learned from your ex-partner: the sort of person she was changed me, the sort of person I was changed her, so we've given each other a gift that we're never going to lose.

Y   You talk about growth. Can you give a definition of growth, because it's clearly a major motive for you.

P   It's really such a hackneyed phrase these days, but to me it's exploiting my potential and I'm only now beginning to realise, in the last couple of years, that I really have unlimited potential and I want to pursue this. I want to explore myself. I want to explore situations and people, and I want to acquire skills and learn. I feel that all of this would have been denied me if I had been trying to do it from the relationship I had because they all would have been potentially threatened. And while my wife would have been saying, 'yes I want you to do all this', she would have been trying to trip me up as well. It would have been making me so insecure. That's what growth is to me – to know that at the end of it all I've given it my best shot and I've risked and I've tried new things.

Y   What would you like to say to anybody reading this book about how to live effectively as a single?

P   I think strive for your own integrity and self-respect. There are periods when there is a lot of pressure being brought to bear upon you by society, by relatives, who would have you believe that what you're doing is not right. There is time when your self-esteem will sink, your confidence will disappear, so you need to nurture yourself and affirm to yourself that what you're doing is right and you're not setting out to try and hurt anybody.

   All you're trying to do is discover yourself.

# DIANE

*D*iane proves the statistic that when one marries young
the odds of the marriage lasting are not great. Married at
19, separated at 20, she is determined to learn from her
traumatic experience. She recognises that before she could
ever again be partnered, she must learn to be successfully
single.

Y  How do you see being single?

D  At the moment I find it to be fairly lonely as I've always
been in a relationship ever since I was 13. I met Mark
when I was 13.

The first thing I did when I left Mark was to leap onto
my brother. I wanted a relationship from him which I'd
never had . . . I'm proud of him. And when he didn't want
me around all the time I had to go through that feeling of
'Oh no he doesn't love me any more', which wasn't true.
I pounced on him because I didn't have anyone, and
because I wanted to have a relationship with him which
I couldn't have while I was with Mark as they didn't get
on.

I've found being single to be good because for once in my life I can do what I want when I want. I haven't had to answer to anybody. I've done more in the last six months than I've ever done in my life. I've travelled overseas. I've taken up a drama and acting course.

I've had to make myself do things as it is easy to sit at home and feel upset. I wasn't upset about leaving the relationship but I was upset I had nobody else to go to.

I decided to plan a few goals for the time ahead. I've achieved most of these goals. I've completely changed much of my life. I was involved with horses from childhood and now I've sold them all, and all my riding gear.

I decided that in leaving the relationship I'd leave everything that I'd had and start completely afresh. I've taken a few singing lessons and I'm going to continue with them. I'm just going to do all the different things I would like to have done and wasn't allowed to do when I was married. For example, I can now spend money on clothing which I was never allowed to do because we were saving for this property in the sky which was never going to happen.

It is hard to be single but it is also fun if you use it in the right way. You've got to keep yourself busy. You've got to put as much time and energy as you can into your work and have an interest in something and create things for yourself.

I still want to be in a relationship one day as I don't like being on my own. But I'm having a good time now and I'm not out looking for somebody. If the right person comes along, well then that's fine, but I'm not wanting to run out and jump straight away into another relationship.

Y   How long was your relationship?
D   I met Mark when I was 13 and we were engaged when I was 16. I was married at 19 and separated at 20. So the marriage lasted a year and a month; the relationship for seven years.
Y   Did marrying change your relationship?
D   Yes. Though it started to change earlier when I began to see the lies he was telling me. But when I was really young I never saw them. They say love is blind and for me it really was. I didn't see what I didn't want to see. I was lucky that I had my parents who realised that things

weren't right. They were very supportive at the same time and let me do what I wanted because they thought that I'd learn from the experience.

I started to realise what was happening when I was about 18 but all I wanted to do was to get married. It was a goal I wanted though I'm not sure why. One reason was probably that the person I was with was a lot older than me. He had been married before and has two children and everyone said to me that he'd never marry again so I was determined that he would. So we were married for the wrong reasons.

Then about six weeks after we married the relationship started going downhill when I found out that he was playing up with someone else. He said he wouldn't any more but he did . . . and he's living with this person now. He also had the attitude when we married of 'now you have to do what I say, I've got you now, I've no chance of losing you, you're going to be here for ever'. And 'you do what I say' which was for me to stay in the house. He didn't want me to have a career as I've always earned more than him.

Once we were married he felt he could treat me as he liked.

Y   It seems to me you've had a lot of opportunity for learning through this relationship – and for growing up.

D   I have learned a lot. I went into the relationship for the wrong reasons and not knowing who I was and what I was doing or what I wanted out of a relationship. Whatever he said sounded OK to me and I went along with it.

I think when I started to stand up for myself he started to back off . . . and to find someone else he could have control over. He also turned to drinking which was a really difficult thing to handle.

Y   How do you think you'd approach a possible next relationship?

D   Very differently. This time I want both of us to have our own individuality. I'd like the person to want to do something of his own because Mark never had any drive of his own. He was always saying he'd been there and done that and he just wanted to settle down and do nothing. I want more out of life.

I had the attitude for a long time that I wouldn't be able

to live without him. I chose to believe that for a while as I didn't want to stand on my own two feet. Now it is vital that I have a basis of trust in a relationship and for my man to do his own thing while I do mine. I want us to be individuals, to be ourselves.

Y  Would you say this to someone right from the outset?

D  Yes. I don't want to lean on anybody and I don't want anyone to lean on me.

Another reason I stayed in the relationship with Mark was the interest we shared in horses. At that time I thought horses were the only thing in my whole life and because he was interested in them too I thought I was very lucky. That fizzled out quickly. It isn't good to base a relationship on a shared interest because it didn't mean anything. I think a lot of people base their relationship on the same interests, both doing the same thing and assume that they therefore must get on well. But that is not necessarily so.

Y  Would you have learned so much if your marriage hadn't been so difficult?

D  Probably not. I think if anyone is deciding to leave a relationship they've got to sit down and decide that they're leaving it for good reasons and think about what they've learned from it. This helps you to get through it. If you leave for impulsive reasons like something hurtful said, you always go back.

The reasons I ultimately left were his playing up and his alcoholism. All the other times that I had left were because I was upset and crying and all I wanted him to do was to say 'I don't want you to leave'. If he didn't say that and I left I would come back two or three days later.

When I really left it was strange. I was calm and cool and I wasn't upset about it. I knew why I was leaving, I'd lost complete respect for him. I didn't cry once. He did. He didn't believe I'd leave him.

Y  What would you say to people who fear leaving a relationship because, as you said earlier, it can be lonely when there's no one there any longer.

D  It is hard to leave. I had to reach the stage of having lost so much respect for Mark that I couldn't stay with him .

Y  Perhaps it was having enough respect for yourself to say 'I can't stay in this negative place'?

**D**   It's hard to say what anyone else should do but if you feel it's right I'd say go for it in every way. Keep yourself occupied for the first few weeks and don't do the same things as before. If they ring back to talk, don't, as you're likely to fall for the same old story and go back. Keep yourself too busy to feel lonely or to grieve.

**Y**   But if you don't grieve, what about the building up of grief inside? Maybe you did yours before you left?

**D**   I did. I cried myself to sleep for more than a year but I just couldn't leave. I was too frightened. I felt I couldn't live without him.

**Y**   Did you have the support of any friends?

**D**   I had already lost most of my friends because Mark didn't get on with them. My parents and my brother and his girlfriend were the ones who helped me through it.

**Y**   On the day you married how did you feel about the relationship and the likelihood of it lasting?

**D**   Funnily enough Mum said to me that morning, 'How do you feel?' I said to her, 'OK and if it doesn't work out I'm young enough to start again'. That was my attitude then so I had doubts from the beginning.

**Y**   It seems as if a lot of the problems were there prior to your choosing to marry and yet you couldn't see them.

**D**   Yes. I remember my father always saying to me 'You're standing too close to the photo, stand back and have a look at the picture because you're too close to the relationship to see what is really happening'. One day I took a step back and I was quite shocked with what I saw.

**Y**   What would you see now as a more important ingredient to people being compatible?

**D**   To not be too concerned with trying to match one another in terms of doing the same things or liking the same things but to respect each other's interests and support each other. To trust one another.

**Y**   When you look to the path before you what do you see?

**D**   It's exciting. I've many things I want to try and fulfil that I haven't had a chance to. I want to do more travelling and to do more acting. I want to expand in different areas. I want to be creative in my work and I'm looking for more challenges. I want another relationship but not a marriage.

# STEVE

*S*teve sees himself as single although he has a stable relationship with his lover. Theirs does not fit the stereotyped view of a 'gay marriage' that emulates the traditional heterosexual couple of husband and wife. He functions as an autonomous but caring individual.

Y  What does being single mean to you?

S  I think my view of being single is a combination of my past experience and of maturing. I think that my attitude at the moment is very peaceful and I'm very direct about where I want to go. To other people I probably have a selfish attitude. But then, because I'm single and because I'm gay I feel as though I've probably got a lot more choices than many other people and can afford to be a little bit more selfish than someone with a family environment or someone in a one-to-one relationship. And I think, too, that there is a distinction between gay relationships and straight relationships . . . something I'd like to talk about later.

I've also felt a lot freer the older I've become. I've a better understanding of myself.

Y  You like yourself more?

S  No, it's more that I understand myself more. I've come to really appreciate friends and my friends have become family. They're a lot closer than natural family. I certainly don't begrudge my life.

   I've had a relationship for the past three years and the one prior to that was for seven. The emotional involvement in those relationships is a continuous one and a learning experience.

Y  When you say you've had those relationships, are you saying that technically you're not exactly single?

S  Emotionally I'm still single because I'm very self-reliant. I live by myself. My current relationship is an understanding relationship. It's a relatively free relationship. I think that living apart adds to it and gives strength to it. We don't live in each other's pockets. We don't often get the chance to grate on each other. We learn to understand each other from a distance while being together often.

Y  Are you free to have other relationships?

S  Well, I don't know that it's that we are 'free' to. There's a tacit understanding. I have, however, had an illicit affair with my first lover for the past two years but that's basically sexual.

Y  So there's a difference?

S  Yes. My present relationship is based on understanding. We live similar lifestyles and we share friends. Our understanding of each other has grown because there wasn't heavy pressure put on us to have a heterosexual-style relationship. It is basically a gay relationship so we're not trying to emulate what straight society looks upon as a couple. For example, my friend is not 'my wife', or 'the girl' and we enjoy that. Once you come to looking at a life shared with someone of the same sex I feel there is no need for role play.

Y  How do you work out who does the domestic chores and those sorts of things?

S  We both do them because we live separately. When we do stay together there's a lot of sharing . . . we both love cooking, we both like entertaining. He's a little more finicky than I am when it comes to house cleaning. There's been a mutual understanding about such things from the word go.

Y  Maybe what you've got is a good model for heterosexual relationships!

S  I'm not sure about that. Despite the fact that I do have this stable relationship, I class myself as a single person because I've arranged my life as a single person and not as having a permanent, bound relationship or a live-in relationship.

Y  Because you are gay have you felt any pressure to live a certain sort of lifestyle? Have you had to carve out your own way?

S  The pressures you feel are society's. I think they're felt by everyone regardless of sexual preference. These days there's a lot more acceptance because there's such a diversity of ways of existing that people are being forced to be tolerant.

Y  There are some myths and ideas about what the gay scene is like. Have you found your identity through these or never felt them?

S  I'm a gay in a very straight environment and I always have been. But I have looked around the scene and I do see the gay cliques but I've not been part of them and I've never thought much of it. Yes, there is a pressure out there but the scene represents a small proportion of gay life.

   I probably do conform to a certain sexual standard. Certainly sex is a great leveller and there is more freedom sexually for the gay community . . . or there was until the AIDS scare. I don't think it is so much a pressure to conform as much as that you do it because that is the way you are. I've read somewhere that gay male sex is easier to come by given you have two males who are aggressive rather than in heterosexual relationships where a male has to chase a passive female.

Y  Do you think that most gay men who are in a stable relationship would still see themselves as single?

S  I know a lot of gay couples who are working very hard at being 'a couple' and several of them are not happy. They're perpetually jealous of each other, they perpetually squabble and fight and they're always pouting or not talking for days on end.

   They're trying to live out a role rather than live out their lives.

   I think two men living together . . . and it could apply

to some women and men living together too . . . must remember that they have their own careers. When you are single and not in a relationship your career becomes paramount. You might well put your career ahead of where a married man with a family can. Two gay males in relationship have to look to their respective careers as well as themselves so there's a lot of self in a gay relationship that can't be avoided. One of the drawbacks is that there will always be that little part of you that you are not able to give.

Y   Are there any disadvantages for you being single?

S   Yes. There's not two of you to buy into a home, to buy a lot of the goods and chattels that couples are able to. You're a one income family. Living a single lifestyle can be costly too, especially if you like the good things of life like I do.

I've always thought it would be nice to meet or to have good friends with whom you could live in a communal environment and have your own space as an alternative to having a very single life, instead of always going back to your apartment or house by yourself. Going back to a very nice place you'd bought as a group where you have your own bedroom and sitting room – your own space – would make it possible to afford more and have company.

Y   What about kids?

S   I suppose I would have liked to have a child but it's never really been an issue because I've been gay since I was 15 and so you just come to the realisation that this is just not going to be. So you don't think about it.

A woman has the choice to bear a child. I've never really had that choice because to me having a child also means having a woman, and this has never really entered the picture apart from one fleeting episode where I was almost engaged by her family.

Y   You could have a child without living with the mother, so it's not a total preclusion.

S   I've never really considered it because it's been my lifestyle to live singly.

Y   What about when you're older? One of the issues that singles face is the possibility of being alone and aged.

S   I've discussed this with mutual friends, gay and straight. We've got each other and I should say that my social group is not gay to the exclusion of anyone else. I have lots of straight friends, probably more than I have gay. We have a certain empathy and live similar lifestyles. We all get along very well and we joke about how when we get old we will live in close proximity or in the same old folks home or whatever. I think that times are changing so rapidly that old age will hold no fear.

Y   Friendships are important to you?

S   Vital. Friendships bolster you. They give you a lot of support. More than a family or a one-to-one relationship could because you've got so many of them. You don't have to burden one person with your problems. You can discuss things with many people and you have a choice.

Y   Do friendships require work?

S   Of course they do. Any relationship be it friendship or a lover relationship always requires time and effort. People expect too much too quickly. In gay society a very important thing is the network of friends that exists that becomes stronger over time, especially in settled gay communities.

I know of one group of gays who have known each other for years and who are now in their fifties. They are an amazingly close-knit group of friends who are just getting older and older together. The older they get the stronger their friendship.

Y   Sex is not the most important thing in gay relationships or your life?

S   Bashing beats, picking up people in bars? No. I think getting a bit on the side is always there, it is always behind your lifestyle. You'll pick up the crumbs wherever you can get them. But it is not overwhelmingly important to the great plan of your life. Your friends are more important. If it comes down to staying home and having a screw or going out with your friends — you'll go out with your friends.

Y   Do you know about loneliness and aloneness?

S   Of course. It's all part and parcel of it. It gives you a chance to explore yourself, to experience emotions. You can be as busy as a bee, frantic, and then come home by yourself and be alone – it's a mixture of everything. And it's a lot of self-reliance too. Despite the fact that you've got your friends you do have to rely on yourself a lot. I think that as a single person you have greater opportunity to experience a broader range of emotions from extreme happiness to loneliness. You learn by it.

Y   What about fear of sexually transmitted diseases?

S   I must admit that AIDS has worried me a bit. It hasn't in my steady relationship because it's fairly monogamous except for my other 'occasionals' but I think it has cut down the type of sex you have and I'm certainly not out and about as much as I was. As I work in health I have more knowledge, I guess, than the usual person about this problem. I certainly use condoms when not with my main friend but I don't carry them around with me as I have little opportunity and don't really want it.

Y   Do you think it has made you more responsible, so to speak, sexually.

S   I think it has come at a time when the self is being a little more aware than the sexual or the urge. Therefore it really hasn't had a great impact in terms of my development. I do feel, however, that my attitude is probably very different to many guys who are doing the scene, going to the bars and the saunas. Especially the young kids who really think that AIDS is an old man's disease or at least an older man's disease and that they don't have to worry about it.

Y   In terms of our conditioning perhaps it is easier and more acceptable to live singly as a gay person than it is for a heterosexual?

S   Yes, I do think that a single male who is not gay would have a much more difficult life because of society's constant pressures.

Y   Research shows that single men are far more at risk of psychological and physical problems than married men. I don't think these figures have been looked at comparing gay single men and not-single gay men.

S   That's an interesting point. Three of my married male friends broke up with their wives in the last year. Greg's marriage ended almost a year ago and he is still an emotional wreck; Frank broke up three weeks ago and is a mess; Martin has been on his own for about six months and he also is an emotional quivering mess. It seems as if their emotional backstop has been pulled right away from them. They've never really had to cope by themselves as a single person and suddenly they have been thrown out by their wives . . . for the three of them, mind you, it was the woman who said 'Go'. These men do not know how to cope with being alone, with not having an emotional backstop, with what to do with themselves in terms of lifestyle.

Y Do they know how to cope practically? Can they boil an egg?

S They'd know how to fix up a house but I doubt that they'd know how to clean one. The crazy thing is that Greg has gone and bought himself a house in suburbia. He's cut himself off from all the sorts of support mechanisms a single person normally has. A single person in suburbia is really isolated. His friends in suburbia are married ... and he feels amazingly left out. It reinforces his sense of loss.

Y And yet the typical gay guy assumes he knows how to live singly.

S That's right. He's had to do it all along. And because he's had to do it all along he has maintained a network of friends and acquaintances that he can rely on for his emotional well-being and so his self-reliance in an emotional sense is greater.

Y It's a very interesting difference.

S Yes, but it's certainly something I've seen. Most gay people I know are relatively happy, well adjusted and 'normal'. I look at these straight people I know who are not managing to live singly and I find them to be mal-adjusted and I couldn't call them 'normal'. There's a lot to be said about the self-reliance of a single person.

Y Lack of ability to communicate and inability to provide companionship have been given as major causes of divorce in a recent survey. How do you as a male relate with women?

S Very well. There's no threat. We talk. I think the only basis of disagreement I have with women are about sexist issues.

Y It seems to be threatening for heterosexual males if the women that they care for have very intimate relationships with men who are gay. Is it because gay men communicate better with women than straight men?

S I think it is because there's no set idea of role and therefore men and women can talk together a lot more readily.

Y What tips would you give to someone reading this book

about how to maximise their life as a single person whether gay or not gay?

S   Being single is a statement of lifestyle rather than a fact of being different. I lead a single lifestyle and it is only a co-incidence that I'm gay.

It's a matter of self, self-reliance, self-esteem and of developing calmness, a realisation that you're in a particular lifestyle through choice or circumstance and that you really should sit back and enjoy it and not try and live an ideal – society's picture – and be made unhappy by it. Realise you're not Robinson Crusoe. Be happy with yourself. It's not an easy thing to do. How you go about it is a very individual thing.

I think it is important to say that to develop a feeling of security in self is not easy. This feeling of contentment has to be worked upon. Quite often living alone or living a single life means that self-confidence can be quite a fragile thing. It involves constant reappraisal, constant bolstering. It requires a very conscious personal effort on everyone's behalf to do that. There's a large amount of self-help involved. I know it is not always easy to find people to bolster that. Counselling can help if you need it. Never be scared to go to a professional if you need it.

Y   A final question. If you were going to paint the ideal scenario for your life over the next few years how would it be?

S   Undergoing my second change of life, meeting new people. Change. Building on the old, starting a different direction and a new job. I would hate to look any further than five years ahead. I'm settled now. I can afford my overseas trip every so often and my comfortable way of life. I have a good life. And I think a good life is made better with good friends.

# A CLOSING THOUGHT

*U*nderlying my philosophy in *Successfully Single* has been my belief that within each of us is an innate urge to grow, to develop until we die. I have named this drive our 'life force', something that gives us individuality, vitality and meaning.

Irrespective of our childhood, we have the ability to overcome the limitations of the past and we can break through the barriers blocking our ability to love.

What has this view of love got to do with being single?

Responsibility is a word that has occurred many times throughout *Successfully Single*. As I see it, it is a word inextricably linked with love – and with loving yourself.

Regardless of whether we are partnered or not, life is full of challenges; the more we are prepared to meet them rather than avoid them, the more likely we are to grow. If we think that being loved by someone will take away the onus of responsibility, we are confusing love for the dependency children have upon their parents. We are fooling ourselves.

Being single gives you the tremendous opportunity for assuming responsibility for yourself, for understanding that only by loving yourself and putting effort into developing your unique potential will you be able to truly love anyone else.

# Source list

Bernard J, *The Future of Marriage*, Penguin, Harmondsworth, 1976

*Bulletin*, The, 'The man shortage: how our best women lose out' 21 May 1985

Burns A, *Breaking Up: Marriage and Separation in Australia*, Nelson, Melbourne, 1980

*Cleo*, 'The Three S Report' March 1985

Dowrick S, *Why Children?*, The Women's Press, London, 1980

Jordan P, *The Effects of Marital Separation on Men 'Men Hurt'*, Family Court of Australia, Principal Registry Research Report No 6

Lynch J, *The Broken Heart, The Medical Consequences of Loneliness*, Harper & Row, Sydney 1979

Mugford S and Lally J, 'Socioeconomic status, gender inequality, women's mental health: some findings from the Canberra Mental Health Survey' *Australian Journal of Social Issues*, 15, 1980, pp30–42

Penman R and Stolk Y, *Not the Marrying Kind: Single Women in Australia*, Penguin, Ringwood, Vic, 1983

Simenauer J and Carroll D, *Singles: The New Americans*, Simon & Schuster, New York, 1982

# INDEX

appearance
  and relationships   22
  and you   80
Arndt, Bettina   20, 21

Bernard, J   33
  *see also* source list
Burns, Ailsa   25
  *see also* source list

Carroll, D   14, 17
  *see also* source list
children
  to have or not to
    have?   121
choices
  about change   70, 98
  about life   11
  about sex   111
  of image   49
  of values   90
  to be single   16, 62
communication
  blocks   84
  lack of   67, 68
  skills   71
contract
  marriage   27
  *see also* marriage
crisis
  identity   26
  mid-life   57

divorce
  and health problems   34
  increase in rate   15
Dowrick, Stephanie   121
  *see also* source list

English, Brian   20

family unit
  changes to   15

fear
  of commitment   107
  of involvement   17
female
  *see* women
friendship
  development of   106
  importance of   94–96
  intimate   9–10, 47, 49, 68

gay
  *see* homosexual
grief   60–61, 132
guidelines
  lack of   12, 48, 55
  write your own   62
guilt   59, 79, 92, 123

health
  *see* well-being
homosexual   18
  *see also* single and
  *see also* relationships
  *see also* male

independence   64–65
individuality
  as I   10
  baby boom, and the   26
  development of   43, 53–71
  loss of   39
  *see also* lifeline
isolation   60, 65, 71, 108
  overcoming   123

Jordan, P   33, 42
  *see also* source list

Lally, J   33
  *see also* source list
lesbian
  *see* single and
  *see* relationships

lifeline
  creating your own  72–79
  make it rewarding  86
  review  99
lifestyle
  according to the media
    marketing  48
  satisfied?  86–90
  successfully single  9
  values to live by  90–91
listening
  active  85
loneliness
  alienated from self  66
  as a single  10
  in relationships  10
  positive face of  105
  post-separation  35
Lynch, J Dr  83, 105
  see also source list

male
  conditioning  31
  disadvantaged  21
  homosexuality  117–118
  living singly  37
  new breed  47
  psychology  34–37
  shortage  20
marriage
  changing age for  16
  contract  27
  gradient  19
  squeeze  20
  why?  24–30
Mugford, S  33
  see also source list

negativity
  emotions  78
  self image  68–69
  stereotypes  39
networking  106

parents — single
  confronting needs of  122
  disadvantaged  22,43
  establishing new
    relationships  61
  house sharing  109
Penman, R  17, 19, 40
  see also source list

relationships
  expectations of  25–30
  homosexual  117–118
  influential  92
  interdependent  66
  lesbian  119–120
  needs from  94–96
  sexual  40
  starting again  36
responsibility
  for one's self  103, 136

sexuality
  see single and
  see parents single
  see choices
  see relationships
Simenauer, J  14, 17
  see also source list
shyness  107
single
  advantages of being  63
  again  128–139
  and aged  140–142
  and health  33
  and homosexual  117–118
  and lesbian  119–120
  and sexual  110–116
  Being Single
    Seminars  54–99
  by choice  16, 62
  but sharing  108
  men  33–37
  stereotypes  12–14

successfully    10
    through circumstance    18,
        62
    through fear    17
    women    38–44
stereotypes
    single    12–14
    negative    39
Stolk, Y    17, 19, 40
    *see also* source list

time
    management of    86–90

values
    *see* lifestyle

well-being
    emotional    83
    physical    80–82
widowed
    *see* grief
women
    and lesbian    119–120
    and single    40
    and solo living    42
    a new breed    45
    conditioning    32, 38–39
    disadvantaged re
        partners    21
    psychology    39
    superwoman    41
    surplus    19
workbook    53
    expectations of Successfully
        Single    58
    expectations of
        yourself    54

## Other CEDAR titles . . .

**Dale Alexander**
The New Arthritis and Common Sense     434 01819 8

**\*Yvonne Allen**
Successfully Single, Successfully Yourself     434 11155 4

**\*Thérèse Bertherat & Carol Bernstein**
The Body Has Its Reasons     434 11138 4

**Frank Bettger**
How I Multiplied My Income & Happiness in Selling     434 11108 2

**\*Judith Brown**
I Only Want What's Best for You     434 11137 6

**Dale Carnegie**
How to Develop Self-Confidence and Influence
   People by Public Speaking     437 95049 2
How to Stop Worrying and Start Living     434 11130 9
How to Win Friends and Influence People     434 11119 8
The Quick & Easy Way to Effective
   Speaking     434 11152 X

**Robert & Marilyn Kriegel**
The C Zone – Peak Performance Under Pressure     434 11121 X

**\*Mildred Newman & Bernard Berkowitz**
How to Be Your Own Best Friend     434 11154 6

**Norman Vincent Peale**
The Amazing Results of Positive Thinking     434 11117 1
Enthusiasm Makes the Difference     434 11136 8
A Guide to Confident Living     434 11128 7
Inspiring Messages for Daily Living     434 11107 4
The Joy of Positive Living     437 95168 5
The New Art of Living     434 11120 1
The Positive Principle Today     434 11112 0
Positive Thoughts for the Day     434 11123 6
The Positive Way to Change Your Life     434 11129 5
\*Power of the Plus Factor     434 11139 2
The Power of Positive Thinking     434 11116 3
The Power of Positive Thinking for Young People     434 11118 X
Stay Alive All Your Life     434 11115 5
The Tough Minded Optimist     434 11135 X
Unlock Your Faith-Power     434 11113 9
You Can If You Think You Can     434 11124 4

**Norman Vincent Peale & Smiley Blanton**
The Art of Real Happiness                              434  11127 9
Faith Is The Answer                                    437  95012 5

**Thomas Quick**
Power Plays the key to performance and success in
   business                                            434  11104 X

**Karin Room**
The New Way to Relax                                   434  11114 7

**Alfred Tack**
Building, Training and Motivating a Sales Force        437  95159 6
Executive Development                                  437  95162 6
How to Increase Your Sales to Industry                 434  11126 0
How to Increase Your Sales by Telephone                434  11111 2
How to Overcome Nervous Tensions and Speak Well
   in Public                                           434  11106 6
How to Succeed as a Sales Manager                      434  11110 4
How to Succeed in Selling                              434  11125 2
Marketing: The Sales Manager's Role                    437  95156 1
1000 Ways to Increase Your Sales                       434  11132 5
Sell Better, Live Better                               434  11109 0

**Judith Tatelbaum**
The Courage to Grieve                                  434  11105 3

**Denis Waitley**
Seeds of Greatness                                     434  11122 8

**\* New in 1988**

# NOTES

# NOTES

# NOTES

# NOTES

# NOTES

# NOTES